The Conversationalist will show you how to make the most of your most important relationships.

—Dr. John Townsend, *New York Times* bestselling author, founder of the Townsend Institute of Leadership

I've seen firsthand that my good friend Russell not only talks about conversations being life-changing opportunities, but he lives it out as well. What an inspiring book and example that Russell gives us!

—Mac Powell, singer, songwriter, producer, and musician of Third Day

The Conversationalist is a primer on how to create deep personal connections. If you follow the principles described by Russell, your own personal and professional influence and connections will grow more quickly and deeply than you can ever imagine.

—Bob Bernatz, Ph.D., corporate psychologist and principal consultant with The Table Group

Russell Verhey is a master teacher. In *The Conversationalist*, he teaches how to build deep, life-giving relationships. This significant book will help you increase your conversational capacity, ask guiding questions, and grow your most important friendships.

—Peter Greer, president and CEO, HOPE International, and author of *The Spiritual Danger of Doing Good*

How many of us wear a sign around our heart that says, *Do Not Disturb*? That is just one of the powerful questions asked by Russell Verhey in *The Conversationalist*. I personally know Russell as a gifted leader, a trusted friend, and a faithful follower of Jesus. I am excited that he has shared his insights into making intentional investments through conversation with a broader audience. Exceedingly rich with wisdom, *The Conversationalist* is for everyone who desires to more significantly practice the power of conversation. Whether a conversation is casual or catalytic, *The Conversationalist* will assist the reader in maximizing the power of the spoken word. In this transformational book, Russell takes us on a practical and at times painful journey into the depths of conversation. Practically informed, Russell will challenge you to abandon a shallow approach to everyday conversation. I highly recommend this book for anyone seeking a deeper, fuller, and richer understanding of the power of life-giving conversation in the midst of a broken world.

—JIMMY DODD, founder and president, PastorServe,
author of *Survive or Thrive: Six Relationships
Every Pastor Needs* and *Pastors Are People Too*

Our life now and our legacy in the life to come are richer if we are skilled in conversing at the heart level with the people in our spheres. *The Conversationalist* will show you how to do this.

—RUSS CROSSON, president and CEO, Ronald Blue & Co.

My good friend Russell is wealthy in what matters most in life relationships. He intentionally invests in other people, as an excellent listener and as a person who really cares. As a result, individuals are drawn closer to each other and closer to their heavenly Father. Apply the truths in these pages and experience the true riches Russell describes so clearly.

—BOYD BAILEY, president,
National Christian Foundation of Georgia

For many years, Russell has modeled the depth of relationship that can come from intentional, catalytic conversations. *The Conversationalist* will give you practical steps to build deeper, more loving relationships one conversation at a time. As you learn to engage others in deep conversations—be it with family, friends, or coworkers—you will also find your own heart growing in love and connection with the people who matter most in your life. For every person in relationship with other people, which pretty much covers the entire human race, this book is a must-read!

—SCOTT AND SUSAN EVANS,
owners of Outreach, Inc.

Those who spend time with Russell Verhey, as I have for several years, know that he models well the message of *The Conversationalist*. This powerful book is one to keep on your desktop so you can refer to it often. It will help you deepen your friendships, enrich your life, and the lives of your family, friends, and colleagues.

—DAVE JEWITT, founder, Your One Degree

Authentic conversations open the heart! One question, one discovery, and one commitment to change multiplied over hundreds, if not thousands, of times can change a world. If you're tired of artificial, canned, and cliché, it's time to try intentional relational engagement. If you desire real change, adventure, and life-defining friendships, Russell will help you get there, one conversation at a time.

—DAN BRITTON, author of *One Word That Will Change Your Life*
and executive vice president of International Ministry
for Fellowship of Christian Athletes

Being fully present is an extraordinary gift to give another person. In *The Conversationalist*, Russell Verhey provides a practical pathway to help you connect on a deeper level with the people in your life. If you want to learn how to cultivate grace and life-giving relationships, this is the book for you!

—TAMI HEIM, president and CEO,
Christian Leadership Alliance

We are excited about *The Conversationalist!* In this age of technology, we have observed families focused on their phones instead of each other, thereby losing sight of the importance conversation can bring to the health and well-being of the family. Allow the proven principles found in *The Conversationalist,* and practiced by our friend Russell Verhey, to help guide and direct you to more meaningful conversations and leave a lasting legacy with your family and friends.

—ED AND RENEE BEHR, owner/partner,
The Platinum Group Realtors, Colorado Springs, CO

THE CONVERSATIONALIST

Building
Life-defining
Relationships
One Conversation
at a Time

RUSSELL VERHEY

BroadStreet
PUBLISHING

BroadStreet Publishing Group, LLC
Racine, Wisconsin, USA
BroadStreetPublishing.com

THE CONVERSATIONALIST: Building Life-Defining Relationships One Conversation at a Time

Copyright © 2016 Russell Verhey

ISBN-13: 978-1-4245-5246-7 (soft cover)
ISBN-13: 978-1-4245-5247-4 (e-book)

Stock or custom editions of BroadStreet Publishing titles may be purchased in bulk for educational, business, ministry, fundraising, or sales promotional use. For information, please e-mail info@broadstreetpublishing.com.

Cover design by Garborg Design at garborgdesign.com
Interior design and typesetting by Katherine Lloyd at theDESKonline.com

Printed in the United States of America

16 17 18 19 20 5 4 3 2 1

The Conversationalist is dedicated to Grandma Helen Gilreath Verhey, who modeled one hundred years of building relationships one conversation at a time. Those conversations will echo for eternity.

CONTENTS

Section Three: The Disciplines of the Conversationalist

INTRODUCTION

My life is a miracle. My mom and dad divorced when I was only three years old. After that time, Dad disappeared from our lives for several years, while Mom tried her best to provide for my one-year-old brother and me.

When I was eight, Mom remarried a violent man with a second-degree black belt in karate, who abused alcohol and my mother on a regular basis. For a while my childhood was marked between sunny summer days and nights of violence and alcohol abuse. Authorities eventually intervened, and he went to prison for the physical abuse he inflicted.

Split between my biological parents, I lived in twelve different homes before I was fourteen years old, all but one of them in Atlanta. During my foundational childhood years I knew the disconnected life—always new neighborhoods and new schools. I was bullied—maybe it was because I didn't have a strong dad around, maybe it was because I was always new, or maybe it was because I was insecure and isolated.

My dad's parents were lovers of Jesus and my eventual safe haven. I spent most of my summers tromping around the woods of their old Civil War home where food and God's love and truth were served in generous abundance. This is where I first learned that there is a better way.

I asked Jesus to come into my heart when I was eight years old on my grandma's wrought iron swing. I knew I needed him if I wanted a different life than the one I experienced at home. The loving conversations with my papa and grandma in the vegetable garden and wood shop shaped me and made me into the man I am today. They read me God's Word and told me how God designed and intended relationships to work and thrive.

During my early teens both Mom and Dad remarried and my home life began to settle. To their credit, my parents encouraged me with an entrepreneurial spirit. They told me, "It's a big world out there! So, go discover and explore a world bigger than the one you've known. You never know what you'll experience or who you'll meet."

At thirteen, my world opened with adventures in backpacking 127 miles on the Appalachian Trail with my uncle Dan. Later that summer at my aunt and uncle's Christian camp in Montana, I had an encounter with God's unconditional love and acceptance. I felt part of a larger family that was connected, cared for, and celebrated. This began a journey of seeking out mentors and godly men in my church, where I had countless conversations around their family tables, witnessing what it meant to be a godly man who loves family and others well. I grew up between the extremes of brokenness and connectedness, fear and faith, which affects how I view relationships today and the conversations that shape them.

My deep conviction that I would live a life of connectedness came on the day of my wedding—January 29, 1994. It was significant not only because I married my best friend and the love of my life, but also for two other reasons. First, that was the first day I heard my dad say that he loved me; and second, as I looked around the sanctuary of the little stone chapel in the North Georgia mountains, I realized my parents didn't have a friend there to celebrate with us.

That day I made a vow to give my life to intentionally investing into relationships, a vow that was made first and foremost with my wife, children, and extended family. What should have been a life marked by brokenness and distrust is now one that is defined by the most meaningful relationships a person could ever have. My life now is the sum of intentional investments into conversations—conversations that have echoed around the world in the richest of friendships, which have blessed me more than any one man should be privileged to enjoy.

I am here to give you hope. I want to encourage you with a greater vision for your relationships as you engage in them by asking life's most important questions, discovering God's highest and best for your life and for those around you. You can live in vibrant, life-giving, life-changing relationships—you are just one conversation away.

A Dream of Connectedness

I have a dream where families stay together, friendships last a lifetime, and leaders serve faithfully within their influence until the next generation succeeds them. It's a dream realized by a movement of conversationalists—people who are more committed to hearing than being heard, serving than being served, and intentionally engaging than living virtually isolated and alone.

I have a dream where people are living out their passions and God-given purposes. I see young people knowing and living out their calling. I see a generation of mentors finishing well, leaving a great legacy, and living their life to the full. I see a world connected in life-defining relationships that will impact it for good. I see the disconnected, disenfranchised, and discouraged invited back into the community of faith, love, and grace. I see the lonely loved and invited into family, friendships formed and fostered over a lifetime, and teams that will be united to make a difference by implementing their vision.

As we live in connected community, we will spur one another on to greater things. We need each other in order to live out our God-given destiny. We cannot live out our calling alone. God intends us to work together, and so we need to talk about our God-given ideas and dreams, fleshing them out in community. It is important that we are able to talk about potential mistakes and pitfalls and how to avoid them. And we need to talk about the best and most efficient ways to accomplish those dreams.

We need great people to rise up in this generation. America has become a modern-day Babylon in need of Daniels, Shadrachs, Meshachs, and Abednegos. We need the William Wilberforces and Hannah Mores of today to right a whole bunch of social evils in our world. We need another Martin Luther King Jr. and Rosa Parks of this generation to have bold faith and turn hearts away from detestable attitudes that separate us from one another. We need passionate evangelists like Billy Graham and prolific Bible teachers like Beth Moore.

William Wilberforce and Hannah More lived in an intentional community called Clapham House so that they could be near each other to discuss their ideas and plans to reform the moral fiber of England. They strategically planned to infiltrate the culture through politics, schools, plays, poems, and pamphlets in order to bring true biblical values back into a country that claimed to be Christian but was living utterly contrary to those values. They knew they needed each other to accomplish such a great task, so their friend Henry Thornton expanded rooms in his house and built other houses to accommodate several households.

By no means am I suggesting that we all need to move next door to each other, but we can learn a tremendous lesson about intentional community. Wilberforce and More had large aspirations to change an entire country, and they knew they couldn't do it alone. The dinnertime discussions, late-night conversations, and chats walking along the path were necessary to formulate the plans and have the courage to stick to it and actually accomplish what they dreamed, despite great opposition and long years to see it become a reality.

What creativity and influence has God given to you? What is the great purpose he wants you to accomplish? Think about C. S. Lewis, J. R. R. Tolkien, and their literary community that wanted to bring biblical concepts and truth to the world of great literature. If it wasn't for their connectedness along the Cherwell River, we would have never read or been inspired by The Chronicles of Narnia and

The Lord of the Rings. Such stories move us not only because of the great mission but also because of connectedness. Even in these fictional stories, friends and family had to rally together in order to see victory; they had to overcome great odds together.

Our world needs countless changes that can only come from people living out their God-intended destiny, and that destiny can only be lived out in connection with others. We cannot live this life to our fullest potential while being isolated and disconnected from each other. The enemy knows that and he wants to keep us feeling alone and rejected. He wants to divide us over silly misunderstandings. He wants us to believe that no one even cares about what we are going through. If he can keep us disconnected and isolated, then he can more easily tempt us into other sins and keep us from living out our God-given destiny.

A Movement of Intentional Engagement

No great movement was ever accomplished in isolation. We are in a day and age where the need is great, but the capacity for greatness is even greater. Everyone has dreams and desires, and many of those aspirations are to make a difference in our world. Yet the way we see change within our families, communities, workplaces, and the world is only through a connected life.

As we are begin this journey together and you move further into the connected life—developing as a conversationalist—your past disconnectedness, brokenness, or failure does not have to keep you bound in shame and regret. You can start today with one relationship, one connection, and one conversation that will put you on the pathway as a conversationalist. Your disappointments hold the potential of divine appointments of friendship that may define your life.

I see you being a part of such a movement—a movement of conversational engagement. Imagine the impact you'd have if you intentionally engaged with just one life-changing conversation. What would be the impact in your marriage? What could happen with your children? What significance would this have for your friendships? And what about the impact on your areas of influence? I want to call you to the challenge today. This challenge will move you beyond your comfort zone. If such a call and challenge feels daunting to you, then you're not alone. It's going to take courage. But I'll be with you along way. It's an honor to be your conversational guide—a coach to help you intentionally engage your most important relationships.

Being a conversationalist means considering and connecting in the world beyond your own. As you do this, you will see a vision fulfilled—a generation of families, friends, and colleagues united for life change. And you may find that the greatest change is your own.

Beginning the Journey

In the spring of 2015, my son Grady and I had the opportunity to go to South Africa with four other dads and sons. After landing at Johannesburg, we took a flight into Zimbabwe. Immediately upon landing at the airport, we quickly observed that the customs, surroundings, and language were quite different. These were beautiful people and an extraordinary land. The thrill of the adventure was exhilarating. The trip was long anticipated from the months of planning and preparation. We were finally ready to be outdoors.

The arid landscape filled with baobab trees was alive. Every corner we turned in the Jeep created new sensations, smells, and sights. The vista point where we first ascended gave us a perspective over the land. It was green, filled with vegetation I'd never seen before, yet it was still a desert. Our guide took us lower into the valley, where we parked near a market and then took a trail into the jungle. The farther we walked, the denser the foliage became. Something shifted in the air—it was no longer dry, but there was now a moisture and a humidity that wasn't present before.

As we turned the corner, I heard it before I could see it—a roar that felt soul-deep. With every step the roar only increased. Our anticipation grew. At the climax of the moment, with the moisture on my face, we turned the corner to an overlook to see one of the most majestic sights I've ever seen in my life. We experienced one of the seven wonders of the world—Victoria Falls.

The water was running at an all-time high. There was mist everywhere. The giddy excitement among the boys and men was a celebration for sure. From nearly every vantage point we saw rainbows, colors that seemed to cut through the mist as the sun shined through. Such a rainbow moved with us on our mile-long hike along the rim of the canyon. There were so many twists and turns in and out of the jungle, every precipice presented a new angle and one of the most majestic sights in the world. With every step we were more saturated in the waters, not from direct flow but rather from the mist that surfaced as a result from the falls. In some cases, the falls were so loud you could hardly hear. It seemed impossible that just a few minutes before we were walking in a high-desert climate filled with sparse vegetation, and now we were surrounded by a jungle—monkeys and other wildlife—in such a beautiful display of creation.

Such a scene set the stage for an experience that will forever mark my life. Being there with my son and other friends was a moment I will never forget, not only for the thunder and roar of the water but for the beauty of such majestic colors found in the rainbows that seemed to track every step. Such is the picture and the possibility for the conversationalist engaging the heart of the listener.

How many of us are surrounded by a desert of relationships but don't realize that we are only a few steps from the roar of a waterfall, an oasis of richness and refreshment that is found in relationship? Solomon wrote, "The purposes of a person's heart are deep waters, but one who has insight draws them out" (Proverbs 20:5). Can you imagine what lies waiting in the reservoirs within your own heart, ready to be drawn out by those in your life? Can you also imagine what it would be like for you to ask the right question that can unlock the reservoirs of life inside your friend, bringing refreshing encouragement?

The Conversationalist is a guide for those who are willing and desirous to go to the edge of the precipice, to look out upon refreshing waters, to feel their mist, and look at the rainbows of possibilities that are present only in the delight of enjoying relationships among good friends. *The Conversationalist* is a call to step out from the desert and into a place of relational refuge. Many, if not all of us, desire such relationships. And yet we must understand that though we desire these kinds of relationships, they actually begin with us.

This book is designed to help guide you into more intentional discovery dialogue that in the end will build life-changing relationships, which will have an impact on you as well as those around you. Come, let's be refreshed by the good waters that hold possibility and refreshment beyond what we can imagine. It's soul-deep, and we can actually feel it before we are able to see it. If you're at a place where you need encouragement today, then I hope you will find it in this book by unlocking the power of conversations that result in true life change.

At the end of the following chapters is a section called Insights and Actions, which is your opportunity to reflect and gain further insights for how you want to grow as a conversationalist. I'll also give you a few recommended actions as you engage in your most important relationships. These are the same questions and exercises I use with leaders, small groups, and teams. Please read them as if you and I were sitting down over coffee, discussing your challenges and goals. As you apply these recommendations, I know they will have the same desired impact I have seen thousands of times. This is my heart for you as you move to the next level as a conversationalist.

INSIGHTS AND ACTIONS

1. As you begin this journey, find a conversationalist partner for encouragement, accountability, and practice. The questions, exercises, and challenges presented at the end of each chapter cannot be done alone. It's about intentional engagement.

2. What kind of conversationalist will you become? Create a conversationalist vision statement. Then write down three specific areas of impact you will have as you commit to intentionally engage your priority relationships in the next year.

3. What difference will it make for you personally, in your family, in your meaningful friendships, and in your workplace? How will that feel?

4. Who are the most important people in your life? Write down their names. Take the first step as a conversationalist and simply let each of them know how you value them and how they are a priority in your life.

SECTION ONE

The Heart of the Conversationalist

We begin with the *heart* of the conversationalist. What resides within your heart will come out in every conversation—whether in words or expression. It's no wonder that ancient wisdom advises us to guard our hearts above all else because "everything you do flows from it" (Proverbs 4:23). Heart preparation must come first, which conversationally sets the environment and will ready you for the potential of life-changing discovery.

Chapter 1

WHY PEOPLE TELL ME THEIR SECRETS

Blessed are those whose strength is in you,
whose hearts are set on pilgrimage.

—*Psalm 84:5*

On a cool summer morning sitting atop a modest knoll that was overlooking a small creek that ran parallel to a railroad line, I listened to my friend tell stories of his childhood in Northern Ireland. Our wives and young kids were busy with their morning activities, and my friend and I were on a pilgrimage retracing some of his childhood roots. We walked a little farther to a ruined platform that once held the structural support for a bridge. Behind us was a small residential area where he once lived and played as a boy; in front of us, across the creek, was a grassy field that represented the peaceful Irish countryside.

My friend pointed out a few other landmarks and then shared with me that this place was once a battleground for war in Northern Ireland during the seventies between Protestants and Catholics. This small creek bed and the bridge that once stood there were scarred by a bomb explosion erupting from the anger and tension of religious and political division. More than any religious perspective or persuasion, for my friend this area was marked by the trauma of families that were separated, communities broken, and people who lost their lives.

That moment marks me in both memory and in friendship. You can begin piecing the stories of people's lives together over coffee-shop conversations and special occasions for dinners, but walking the ground where they once walked at defining moments in their life takes a relationship to a whole other depth. The sights, the sounds, the smells, the landscape, the colors of the season—all of those things set the environment. The joy of that memory is that we didn't stay in that place, but we continued our travels, building new memories, going new places with fun and laughter. By the end of our trip, we were dreaming about what was ahead. The joy for me is that some of those whispered dreams have become a reality that have impacted people's lives all over the world.

Why would my friend entrust me with his life story? What endears someone to open up the past so that it shapes the hopes for the future? What builds such a trust and confidence? How do I engage conversationally to capture a moment like this? And how will I respond to honor his story and the gift of friendship?

A Conversationalist Connects

As a conversationalist, I find that everything begins with connection. I am often asked why people tell me their secrets, and the simplest answer I can give is that I take the time to walk alongside people, to be in proximity during the moments when they are asking questions, and to engage in dialogue with them. People tell me their secrets because I take the time to care, to listen, and to recognize and reflect on where they have been, where they stand today, and where their hopes are for tomorrow.

The work of the conversationalist invites a person to look around at the landscape of life and engage his or her relationships. It invites a person to be more intentional and connect, to nurture the relationships that have been neglected, and to deepen the relationships that may have plateaued. It's to guide an individual into a greater awareness and discernment of the people who are in one's life and who are on the cusp of a life-changing moment. And such a decision may only be waiting for a life-changing conversation to happen. Whether or not you feel you have the right skill set to guide a conversation to a defining decision that may change the trajectory of someone's life for good, know that you have the potential to encourage relationships.

The intensity that you develop as a conversationalist will be equal to how people inspire you. You can care, value, and even love, and yet these endearments start with a spark, much like a first date. Connection comes from how fascinated you are with the stories of others' lives and how curious you are with the details of their journey. Connection comes by entering into a conversation that leads to a discovery process in which you're not really sure where it is going to end, yet you want to be one of those who are along for the ride.

If you want to grow in meaningful relationships, then you can do so by being a witness to people's life-defining moments. Such moments happen around us all the time, yet we may be disconnected from what is actually taking place. But taking the time for a few well-meaning conversations may make all the difference in their lives (and even in ours). If we are to grow as conversationalists, then we will have to develop as guides, and skillfully grow in our ability to have such conversations in the relationships that will define our lives and theirs.

In this day of social media, where people ironically feel more disconnected than ever before, it is my hope that we would be people who are interested in more than just news, weather, and sports. It is my hope that we would gracefully guide conversations where they need to go, that we would lead people into a discovery of all God intended and all they hope to become. The result of their thinking, consideration, and dialogue would prompt them to take action on what matters most in their lives, and that the impact of those commitments would change their lives as well as the lives of those within their influence.

Defining a Conversationalist

The dictionary would define a conversationalist as a person who enjoys and contributes to good conversation or an interesting person in conversation. But I would take it a step further and say that a conversationalist is one who considers "how . . . [to] spur one another on toward love and good deeds" (Hebrews 10:24). How do we become a conversationalist? We do so by listening to the secrets of someone's story, celebrating their present reality, and then considering their future possibilities.

My early perception of a conversationalist is one who could come in with a few bits of information, be able to wax eloquent in any variety of topics—entertaining with story, speculating with questions, and reciting facts and figures, maybe even some poetry—and would create awe in those who were listening. The more I thought about my perception, however, the more I realized that it was really one of an orator, not a conversationalist. Such a brilliant communicator knows the audience, and they are able to present their talk in a way that connects, leads them along, and invites them into the story.

On further reflection, I realized a conversationalist does more than entertain or wow by their knowledge or experience. A conversationalist speaks more to the heart of the matter, surfacing the most important issues in an individual's life. He doesn't so much present what he knows, but he helps draw out and discover what others know and what God has placed in their heart and brings them into the discussion. Whether it's one-on-one, in a small group, in a classroom setting, or in an organizational context, a conversationalist draws out the best of the people participating in the dialogue.

The conversationalist is like a skilled facilitator who knows the people—their values, their priorities, and maybe even some of their past. She is one who asks questions to invite others to fully be a part of the conversation. The conversationalist may also be aware of the present challenges a person is going through, knowing that the people involved may be stymied from past decisions or circumstances. Rather than being crippled by challenges, he or she can draw out the wisdom of learnings as insights into exploring possibilities for future opportunities. The conversationalist invites a new perspective that is shaped by all the voices participating, through a mutual discovery that can only be done collectively within trusted circles.

Have you ever sat with a conversationalist? Have you ever sat with someone who brings out the very best in you? Or have you ever been a part of a team environment that may be stagnant, and a person comes in, and by a few comments and questions shifts the air in the room and brings an energy and a life that wasn't present before? It's more than just charisma or personality that is at work; it comes from the heart of the conversationalist who takes time to consider the needs and interests of those around him, what moves them, what stirs their heart, and what spurs them on. And the result of such a conversation moves the people present to do the same for others.

I am a conversationalist not so people can enjoy engaging conversation with me, but so they can discover what God has placed in their heart and live it out with passion. I am not a conversationalist who has arrived, but rather one who is on the journey to becoming better. The ideals, principles, and models presented in these pages help stimulate me. What does it look like to aspire to be a conversationalist? There is a resolve to wake up on a daily basis, to listen to God, and intentionally engage others.

God designed us to live connected to him and to others.

For you to declare yourself a conversationalist is to evaluate the kind of relationships you hope to build, the kind of friendships you hope to foster, and the kind of family you hope to create. The vision of the types of relationships you hope to attain will condition you for the kind of conversationalist you hope to become. Whether you consider yourself an introvert or an extrovert, it makes no differ-ence at all—we all have relationships.

Whether our relationships are many or few, to engage relation-ally is to be human, and to isolate ourselves would be like limiting the oxygen we breathe. God designed us to live connected to him and to others. Our connecting point to develop such relationships is through each and every conversation we engage in. As conversa-tionalists, let us consider "how we may spur one another on toward love and good deeds" (Hebrews 10:24).

An Open Invitation

"You can ask me anything you want. My life is an open book." There are times when I feel like one of the wealthiest people on the planet, relationally speaking—I am so grateful for the friends I have in my life. Yet no matter how many people I know around the world, those people who have access to my heart seem to be few. We don't get access to one another's lives just because we have a great idea, an opinion, or a preference. We move beyond everyday conversations with permission. It is such a simple idea, yet I can assure you that it is so rare that every time it is exercised it is well received.

Permission honors the relationship and creates the potential for meaningful engagement, whether in the moment or in the future. Permission is more than just a good idea or practice. In fact, my life has been shaped by this, having it modeled for me at an early age by my good friend Peter. We were sitting at a men's retreat in the fall of 1993. I had just gotten engaged to Cari, while Peter had been married just over four years, and he was more than happy to pass along anything he had learned along the way. Clearly, I seemed to be struggling over my words and the questions to ask when Peter stopped my stumbling and said, "Russell, you can ask me anything you want. My life is an open book."

For the first time in my life I had a friend who had given me access to anything and everything I wanted to know about his life, from his upbringing, school days, his work life, his marriage, and even his hopes and dreams for the future. I don't remember the exact details of what we talked about that night, but I clearly remember a man who vested himself in me and gave me permission to ask anything. *I was limited only by the questions I didn't know to ask.* That was a defining point in the conversation, as well as a friendship that has lasted almost twenty-five years. The joy for me is that after all these years, I still have permission to ask anything I want.

Imagine for a moment what granting permission would do for you relationally. It is such a simple statement, yet it is filled with potential risk, exposure, and maybe even a sense of loss if something about your life is revealed. On the other hand, what does this do for the possibility of a life-defining relationship? And what could you discover in a friendship that could never be revealed without permission? Not everyone has access and permission to my heart—this is only reserved for a select few—yet not giving permission to a few people will limit the potential of some extraordinary relationships.

I recently sat down with Tim, a man in his sixties and who is a licensed counselor and therapist, primarily for marriages. He helps couples through thirty-hour intensives to see their marriages fully restored, witnessing relational miracles all the time. We have had many chats over the years, but this was our first time together in a private setting. We were catching up, and somewhere in the course of getting to know each other deeper, Tim began to ask a question and then stumbled a bit, perhaps feeling like it was inappropriate. I reassured him: "Tim, you can ask me any question you want. My life is an open book."

With that comment, even with fork in hand and a mouthful of food, he stopped chewing and his mouth dropped as he stared at me. Given his trade in marriage counseling and the strong statement of trust and permission, he said to me, almost in a state of shock, "Russell, do you have any idea how rare it is that you would say that?"

His comments that followed made me feel like we had moved years ahead in our friendship in just a few short hours. Again, permission is not for everyone in our life, but by giving it to the few, they will be able to take us further than we could ever imagine.

Navigating Expectations

I didn't wake up one day and decide I was going to be a conversationalist. I have probably asked more annoying questions in my lifetime than meaningful ones. My children have an unusual amount of grace when I keep pressing them with questions when clearly they need a pause from the conversation. My oldest, Ellie, even uses a hand signal, saying, "Hang loose, Dad," meaning, "I'm good for now, so lighten up."

As a conversationalist, you can quickly exhaust your welcome if you don't know the boundary lines of appropriate questions. You've overextended your stay beyond the water cooler or a ninety-minute lunch when the look in the other person's eyes says, "I have had so much, I need to take some time to digest." Like a really good meal, after you have taken time to enjoy it, then you have to get up from the table and move around a bit before you can take in any more. The conversationalist knows the grace of their welcome; therefore, navigating questions is a critical component of being a great conversationalist.

You're on a pathway of guiding the conversation to a personal discovery, taking time to consider what moves the other person. Getting a list of fifty questions to ask can be a little overkill, let alone ridiculous. You should take the time to consider the most important questions you should be asking. In the consideration of such questions, you are prepared before you ever meet with someone. Three or four well-crafted questions can easily take a half hour to a couple hours to work through. Certainly, questions stimulate other questions, yet you anchor your time on the key questions that help move the conversation (and thus the relationship) forward.

Intentionally engaging relationship is a press. By that, I mean every time you ask a question, it potentially poses a risk that maybe you've gone too far or you've asked a question that there is not an answer to, and you have to sit in a few moments of awkward silence trying to figure out where to go next. As a conversationalist, your role as a guide is just as important as the grace in making people feel welcome and at ease in moving through the dialogue.

While navigating expectations, you will find the balance and tension between pressing with questions but not pressuring for answers before it's time. Really great questions, well timed in an environment of grace, don't always have to demand answers. The greater the question can often mean the greater the ambiguity of the answer. And, in time, whether it's in the moment or over a series of conversations, such ambiguity may lead to a clarity that results in a change of trajectory in someone's life. One of the greatest joys as a conversationalist is that you get to be a witness to these early musings that set a course for new actions in an individual's life.

Asking Questions

The reason people tell me their secrets is simply because I take the time to ask. Henry Thoreau once wrote, "I had the best day of my life because someone took time to listen to me." I was on a call with a leader who has become my friend only in the past year. As we discussed some of the ideas around this book, he shared, "Other than my wife, I really have only one or two friends I talk to at this level. I consider myself a good friend to many, and I am blessed with a lot of great relationships, but the fact is we just don't take the time to get beyond the normal conversations of every day. I am thankful I have at least a couple people I can talk to at this level, but I know I need to do a better job of taking the initiative to press a little further with some of my key friends."

> The reason people tell me their secrets is simply because I take the time to ask.

When you are talking on an intimate level, it's more than just the stigma of what you are hiding. Rather, it could be something that you have not had the opportunity to share simply because somebody hasn't taken the time to listen. Take a moment to conversationally acknowledge the sacred privilege of being invited into dialogue at this level. Whether the ideas are clearly defined or you're just exploring them for the first time, recognize that you are talking at a level that is uncommon and that leads to some uncommon discoveries along the way.

How do you know when you've crossed over the threshold to uncommon conversations? You can train your ear for keywords that give you an indication that you are getting close or that you have arrived: *dreams* and *fears*, *desires* and *disappointments*, *hopes* and *heartache*, *love* and *loss*. These words are not exhaustive by any means, but they do represent four talking points where you know you are working at a heart level. This is not common, everyday conversation; it is reserved for special moments. As a conversationalist, you have the opportunity to steward such moments and to guide the conversation in order to further define these areas in the context of others' lives.

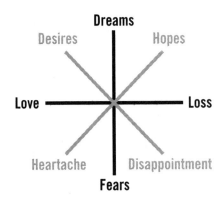

Notice the tension between each of these four areas. They represent the extremes of what people may feel, think, and act upon for good or for bad. Like any good story, we hang on the tension of these moments. It's the arc in the script that makes a great story.

Our life is not made up of all mountaintop moments, nor should it be exclusively in the valley either. When we are in these sacred places conversationally, we are talking at levels we may think are only reserved for the therapist's office. So often, the tension of these hard times before the good comes causes us to jettison the conversation because we truly don't know how to engage. Our role sometimes is just to sit quietly in the pause of the conversation through a difficult time. But as people walk through that valley and climb to the mountaintop of their dreams, desires, and hopes, and experience the love within their relationships, it is extraordinary. And it is that which adds richness to relationships because we have stood through the good and the bad.

Isn't that what we all long for? Isn't that what we are made for? Yet so many people are void of these kinds of relationships, where they have exchanged the richness of walking through the sacred moments of their lives for a virtual life where they experience people in an artificial way. These uncommon conversations shared in trusted moments are not a burden but a blessing, and they should be embraced with joy even though there may be tensions of the unknown.

Creating Space for Uncommon Conversations

Imagine for a moment if you and I were beachside at your favorite coastal vacation spot. You had just finished a long walk after an afternoon of play with the kids. And when you get back to the house, you grab a drink before dinner to watch the sunset. You and I visit a little bit, talking about what a refreshment it has been enjoying a few days out of the normal rhythms of work and other commitments. You're really at a place of the most rest you have felt in months if not years, and then I ask, "If we were to come back here three years from now, where do you hope to see your life? What will you have done with your family and the friendships in your life during that time?"

As you begin to share your answer, you may have moments where you are smiling, exhibiting a real sense of joy as you think about the possibility of a dream coming true. Yet within a few minutes the conversation may take a quick turn, where it may evoke fear of some regret or hurt that you hope will be made right. If we were to talk for an hour and I would have the freedom to ask questions about the things you shared, we would be in a space of true honor as we listen at a level that may have never been shared.

More often than not, such moments won't happen beachside. But during the normal course of your week, you may encounter a pause in the conversation where a seemingly minor comment reveals a heart-level expression of what matters most to the person you are talking to. As a conversationalist, you have the opportunity to engage in such moments to acknowledge rather than deflect. You can simply seize these moments with a comment like, "Wow, that sounds fascinating! Tell me more about that." By doing so, you are inviting your friend into a deeper relationship. As you look for such moments, pay attention to the cues of someone's dreams, desires, hopes, and what they love, which invites a dialogue around those thoughts and ideas.

When you see signs of such moments, you have a decision to make: to press in or to pull back, to ignore or to engage. It may not be in that moment, but it could be an acknowledgement later in the elevator or in the parking lot at the office that says, "I remember what you said yesterday in that meeting," or, "At dinner last night, what you shared really hit me and I'd love to hear more about it." Comments like these honor that person amid the stale mundane of everyday life. Your acknowledgement shows that you are paying attention, which opens the door for further discussion, creating space for more uncommon conversations to take place.

Characteristics of the Conversationalist

As a conversationalist, you'll want to conversationally develop as a guide who will spur on life-changing relationships. So you must ask yourself, "Why would somebody tell me their secrets?" Maybe you feel like those are conversations reserved for someone special, or at least they are private thoughts should be shared with anyone but you. "Why would somebody reveal to me what matters most to them? I may not feel like I'm deserving of their trust or confidence, and the truth is that I really struggle with my own insecurities within my friendships. I look around at people who seem to be so fulfilled in their friendships, and I always feel like I am lacking. Yet I am not sure how to be a better conversationalist." If you are in that place today, you can develop such confidence that someone would entrust their story to you.

You can come up with the best questions in the world, but if you don't have the connection and the confidence of those you are engaging with, then your question may fall on deaf ears. I have wrestled with the desire to build my conversation skills beyond an intrinsic gut feeling to explicit characteristics that I can share with others to help cultivate a confidence to move beyond just news, weather, and sports. After considering dozens, I would suggest three primary attributes that build confidence in relationships: safety, belief, and help.

Safety: I Am Here for You

First of all, you need to come from a place of peace and rest. If your life is characterized by anxiety and fear, then people will not feel safe around you. However, when you have stability in your life, then you become an anchor to help ground others. When people are feeling vulnerable to whatever they are facing, they need someone to lean on. You must be able to set aside your own agenda and motivations, because people are looking for an encouraging, judgment-free sounding board. That is not to say you don't speak truth when it's needed, but it's always done in love. No matter what you say, the other person will still feel loved because of how you say it. You must come from a spirit of humility with an attitude to serve.

It's not about you and your story but about truly listening to the other person in that moment.

Everyone has challenges. In fact, I've never met a person who doesn't have their fair share of trials and difficulties. The issue has more to do with how you respond to those challenges—through uncertainty there is a strength to your life that is marked by peace. My pastor often asks, "Do you have war in your heart? Do you come into relationship always wanting to pick a fight? Do you have an insatiable desire to win, no matter the cost? Or do you pick your battles for the sake of relationship?"

As you have a desire to grow as a conversationalist, people must experience you as a safe person. No matter how secure or insecure a person is, either because of external circumstances or internal wrestling, most people have a well-tuned instinct of whether you are a safe person. It is critically important to understand the idea of safety in terms of relationships if you are to grow as a guide in conversations. Do you represent a certain level of objectivity to that person, or do you come with a certain bias or agenda?

We see this in family dynamics all of the time. As we all know, family members love us but their counsel is not always the most objective. The same would be true in a work setting where, because of our role and responsibility, our boss has to keep us accountable for our performance in the workplace. Such a person in authority may have a conflict of interest to our needs and desires; however, we should not make excuses for our position within an organization, a church, or even a family at the expense of extending the peace in our lives to others.

If you do not have peace to give, then others may be resistant to sharing beyond what's necessary to maintain a relationship. If this is an area of significant struggle for you, one of the first steps you can take is to find people who are safe in your own life—find people who represent a significant amount of peace, no matter what they have faced circumstantially—and then spend some time with those people and learn from their ways.

Belief: I Believe in You

The greater the dream, the greater the fear. As people entrust you with their dreams and hopes, their fears are only a whisper away. The truth is that fear and dreams are usually interwoven. Even the greatest leaders still struggle with a chronic condition of self-doubt. Deep within our psyche we wonder, "Can I do this? Do I have what it takes? Will I endure to the end?" These are massive thematic questions that war in the soul.

Though our dreams and plans may propel us forward, we often trip up on our own second-guessing. In these defining crossroad moments, what often makes the difference of whether we go forward or retreat is whether we have people in our lives who say, "Go for it! I believe in you." The energy and courage it takes to whisper a dream, let alone proclaim it from the rooftops, somehow leaves us defenseless to the crippling doubt.

It's the people in whom we have confidence and trust that we lean into during these moments. If they say we can do it, we trust them, maybe even more than we do ourselves. This is the voice of encouragement that considers how to spur one another on toward love and good deeds and that believes in them more than they believe in themselves. The fact is everyone wrestles with the devices that would cause us to stumble in doubt, shame, regret, and fear. Each of these have their place to keep us level-headed with a healthy caution, but if left unchecked they can cripple us to inaction.

As a conversationalist, one of the most influential roles you can play is to simply say, "I believe in you! Go for it! I am with you!" Hearing that propels the other person forward to action beyond what their self-doubt would allow. As with safety, if you want to grow as a conversationalist, then extend your belief and a courageous spirit to those in your life. If you lack such skill, then tap into those people who have believed in you. Who are those people who have moved you forward? As you spend time with them, see what resonates with you. If you don't have access to them, then reflect on the times where you did and what it felt like to be in their presence. Learn from their ways and then go exhibit the same.

Help: Let's Find a Way

As a conversationalist, you spend time with people, speaking into their lives but also listening to their heart. The opportunity will arise for you to help—it may be in the form of timely counsel, introducing them to a connection with someone else who can help them, or sponsoring them till they get on their feet once again. Help doesn't always mean being the checkbook and the resource of their dreams. You can be an advocate for them without always being the answer to the problem. The work of the conversationalist is as a guide who will help strengthen another to the point where they can get up and walk on their own two feet, with the hope that one day they will do the same for others.

When somebody is entrusting their ideas and hopes for the future into your care, it is usually because they feel stuck. They may feel a sense of fog or fatigue, or they may have simply lost their way. They may have reached out toward their dreams and have been met with great disappointment. As you sit with someone who is disillusioned with where they are at in life, your role as a conversationalist is to help them explore and discover a new way forward.

As you exhibit the characteristics of safety, belief, and help, the word will get out. Your reputation will proceed you, and you will be known and trusted within your circle of influence. As you look for opportunities to create space, taking conversations to the next level, people's lives will be impacted. As you gracefully press in without pressuring, you are going to see a difference in your relationships. Inviting those to ask anything they want, you will move into a select few of friends, being entrusted with their stories, affirming them and encouraging them to move forward. You will be known as a conversationalist.

Not a Goal to Strive Toward

Why people tell their secrets, revealing what matters most in their life, is not some goal to strive toward or a sense of accomplishment that we have arrived conversationally. Rather, it is just an indicator of people's confidence in us. Do you carry the confidence of your friends and family? Why or why not? What changes do you need to make in your life that will help you become a safer person who exhibits peace? And when people spend time with you, how do they know you are for them and believe in them? Can you help find a way toward their dreams and to even overcoming their fears? It can be as simple as clearing the fog of doubt to the point of finding the first step they need to take in the right direction.

This book proposes seven life-changing questions where, as you set the environment within your relationships and hold the confidence of those people in your life, you will begin to warm up to the possibilities and experience the discovery of the answer that can change people's lives. You certainly have thoughts and ideas of your own, but people take action more on what they realize and discover for themselves than answers that are prescribed for them. And how we get there is through asking meaningful questions.

These seven questions represent seven areas of life that help you live out your purpose, express your passion, and define the priorities of your life. But there is so much more than just launching these questions into a discussion. Much of the work of the conversationalist is the art of knowing the right question to ask at the right time. We need to first explore the heart preparation for seeing everyday conversations turned into God appointments. However imperfect these thoughts are, I hope that the ideas and stories within these pages will spur you on relationally, taking your friendships deeper. The secrets of your future are waiting to be revealed with every conversation.

Insights and Actions

1. Who is someone in your life who is safe, believes in you, and who will help you along your way?
2. Describe your relationship with that person and his or her significance in your life.
3. What keeps people from entrusting their stories to you? What can you do to change that?
4. What would the impact be if people were confident that you are safe, that you believe in them, and that you will help them?

Chapter 2

Navigating the Five Levels of Significant Conversations

The landscape of conversations is a lot like the landscape of the Colorado mountains. You can climb through some valley that looks as if no one has ever set foot in that place before, and as you continue to follow a creek bed you come over a rise and see a beautiful oasis of a hidden lake surrounded by aspen trees and Colorado wildflowers in the high country. It's a place of refreshment, inviting you to linger and enjoy. After your respite, you then continue your climb to the ridgeline. It gets steeper, and the trail starts using switchbacks. You're wondering if you're even going in the right direction.

It's a hard push. The higher you go, the trail to the top becomes more unclear; yet as you navigate to the ridgeline, you cross over the precipice. You turn the corner and you finally see it—a view you have never seen before. Climbing to the summit, all you can see is the hill that is yet to climb, and then suddenly your whole world is opened up. If you've ever hiked or explored before, especially in unknown places, then you know what I am talking about.

Likewise, when you're navigating considerable conversations with someone, maybe for the first time, it's a lot like our trail to the peak of the mountain. So often in conversations, we are lost in the valley of the unknown, knowing there's still more and we're not quite to the pinnacle of perspective, but for one reason or another we stop short of the top.

For my fellow hikers and climbers, you will be familiar with a topographical map. And from that map you can get your bearings, see where you've been and where you're headed. You can also see the contours and the elevation change based on the circles as they narrow toward the top. The five levels of significant conversations are a lot like these contours to the map—they are a pathway to life change.

Every day, we have the opportunity to engage with people at varying degrees. As a conversationalist, as we grow and mature, we're invited into greater levels of meaningful dialogue that have the potential for life-changing implications. Those five levels of significance are casual, contextual, conceptual, considerable, and catalytic.

Moving to the Next Level

A friend of mine, John, is one of these guys who, when you first meet him, is larger than life. It's more than just a charismatic personality that's attractive; his sincerity draws you in. John is a family man who loves his wife and kids like crazy. He is also a high intensity charger in his work life, and he found his sweet spot when he landed in the seat of a fighter jet serving in the US Navy. When he retired from the Navy, he went into corporate life where he worked in the legal industry, bringing in multimillion-dollar deals as a VP of business development.

A few years ago, however, something tragic happened. He was out on a ranch in Montana riding horseback when the ten-year-old stallion that had only recently been broken threw him, resulting in a life-threatening accident. Some twenty surgeries later and after two years of recovery, John can only work part-time. Today, when you marry his personality with his past, he is a guy who doesn't take life for granted. He lives from a passion, a sincerity, and an intensity. John and I have had many meaningful conversations over the last several years; most of them are casual, but with time they've moved to greater levels of significance.

John has some significant decisions he needs to make, not so much in regard to his lack but to his abundant opportunities. This means that he has to narrow his focus and choose. He spent an entire day for a personal planning retreat just to get settled so he could make some important decisions. I had the privilege to talk with him the morning after his retreat, while he was at the cusp of a catalytic moment. It's the context of this story that really illustrates the need to understand the levels of significant conversations.

Before we step into the circles of significance, I want to acknowledge the readers who may be thinking, "Russell, I've never had a conversation like the one you've described. I've never engaged in that level of dialogue, nor have I had anyone engage with me at this level either." But this is the very heart of the conversationalist.

You can't impart what you don't possess. If you haven't received something, then it is extremely hard to give it away to others. For those of you who may feel timid, unsure, or insecure, there are catalytic conversations waiting to be had by people in your circle. You just have to be willing to go there.

For those of you who may be wondering, "Why would I want to engage in that level of dialogue?" then I want to remind you of a passage from Proverbs 11:25: "A generous person will prosper; whoever refreshes others will be refreshed." Real, sincere, authentic, life-changing conversations are rare, and when you have the opportunity to engage in them at this level, there is a refreshment and a renewal that happens. When you press forward with a meaningful question that unlocks a life-giving exchange, then you open your own life to be refreshed just as you are in the act of refreshing another.

Whenever a point is raised or an idea is presented, our natural inclination is to consider the answer for ourselves. For the conversationalist, however, we take it a step further, asking ourselves,

"How do we engage with this idea for other people in our lives?" As we move forward into these levels of trusted and sacred dialogue, we are moving into a realm of friendship that is rare.

When we are at defining moments in our life, it becomes clear who our true friends really are. If we are experiencing a season of loneliness or isolation, there's likely to be walls raised high with Do Not Disturb signs on the doors of our hearts. However, if we're ready to break down isolation, if we're ready to move forward and deeper into friendship, then we can move from casual conversations to catalytic moments where we have the opportunity to facilitate and to be a witness to life-changing moments and decisions.

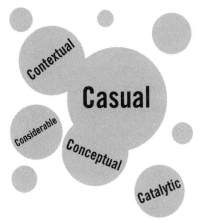

Levels of Significance

Level #1: Casual Conversations— Importance of the Small Things

The idea that conversations should move beyond more than news, weather, and sports suggests that there's not a value in these three talking points. I often hear from people who just want to be with others whom they can go deep with. Ironically, those are the same people who don't go deep with anybody because they aren't around anyone. They may throw around some comments like, "They are so superficial," or, "What a fake," or, "I just wish that person could be more real." But when we're talking about casual conversations, we are not talking about being hypocritical. No, we're talking about the art of beginning good conversations so that within a few moments we have an opportunity to make a first impression that gives both parties an indication of whether or not they want to move forward in their conversation. Casual conversations also help find common points in what can be the early foundation for a sincere relationship.

It's amazing how offering a few comments and a couple questions within moments of meeting somebody for the first time can set him or her at ease, which allows everyone to feel relaxed and at home in the relationship (which in turn encourages everyone to let their guards down). Casual conversations really are an art. Most people I know have an unbelievable instinct when meeting somebody for the first time—they have an amazing sense of whether that person has an agenda for the conversation. When that sincere agenda is there, then the conversation can continue to build up and encourage each party.

Casual is cultural. We've seen scenes in movies where a young man comes to the family dinner for holidays for the very first time, trying to figure out acceptable behavior, let alone the questions to ask. Watching this is comical because we can all relate to it and how awkward it feels to be the person on display, feeling like we are going to say or do the wrong thing.

Casual conversations go beyond just first impressions. If we are to nurture those relationships we have deep history and trust with, then we must learn to nurture them by knowing the appropriate level of casual interaction till the relationships are ready to go to the next level. Just because of the culture of my family, I've experienced nearly twenty-five years of watching my wife interact with her sister over the casual details of each woman's day. Sometimes I am amazed by how much detail they can talk about related to the normal course of their everyday activities. They illustrate the point that the details are important, but much more important is that every minute people talk about the specifics of their lives—what they think, what they feel, what's going on—they express love and care for one another.

There is great value in the casual side of relationships, the nurturing and building up of one another just by relating the stories of our everyday existence. One of the greatest gifts of marriage is that our spouse is a witness to our life. Though I'll never be able to relate with the level of detail that my wife shares with her sister, I can still celebrate in some of the casual details of her day. So whether it's a long-term relationship or a first-time conversation, we can be intentional with having meaningful conversations when it comes to the casual aspects of someone's life. It is these moments that nurture and ready the relationship to move to the next level.

Level #2: Contextual Conversations— Perspective of the World Around Us

When Pete called for some friends to come to the hospital to support him in prayer for the healing of his daughter, she had already been in the hospital for four days. At her birth, little Emma was given up and then moved into the foster system. She spent the first 5–6 months in the hospital without the nurturing care of a mother or father. She was born one day after what hospital regulations would allow to sustain the life of a premature baby. She weighed only a pound and a half when she was born, and now at two years old she continued to struggle with her breathing, and she had to use oxygen during some portion of most of her days. And now this little one was in the hospital once again with pneumonia and a host of other issues.

Context is everything. In fact, context is a conversational filter. It helps you know your part to play in the story. There was no question of whether or not I would come to the hospital to be with Pete, his wife, and his little girl. Why is this? First, I deeply care about Pete and his family. But there is also the fact that his story intersects with my story. Ten years ago, I was in a a baby house in little town on the outskirts of Samara, Russia, a thousand miles east of Moscow. Here's where I first met my little boy, who at nine months old had hollow eyes from being underfed and underloved. I know the power of support from fellow friends and family coming alongside, battling in sickness and health, especially friends and family with an adoption story.

When we learn the story about someone's life, it adds a weight to the relationship. It is also an invitation for us to go further and deeper with that person, especially if we have a point of common ground. Pete and I are also bonded because we share an adoption story as parents. It just so happens that one of the guys in that room, and his wife, were considering adoption. Context is the invitation for the next level of significance in a relationship.

Context certainly does not have to be life-implicating circumstances; it could be expressed by clarifying expectations. I have a business associate in the financial world who always has the same opening line within the first couple of minutes of our time together: "What do you hope to accomplish from our time together?" His question is direct, yet it is still open-ended and allows me to express the details of any agenda or expectations I have. If there is something I am hesitating about sharing with him, his question may give me the push that I need. If the invitation wasn't there, I might hold back until another meeting.

Have you ever noticed, when you're in conversation with someone, that as it moves from the casual to the specific details of what's happening in a person's life, you have greater insight and perspective? This is because you're learning more about the influences that are impacting them, allowing you to be more empathetic toward them and their situation. Such conversations allow us to care at greater levels, so that we can show love and express compassion—which may be exactly what that person needed in that moment.

When do we know the conversation needs to go to the next level: from contextual to conceptual? It's when a conversation needs a fuller scope of what's happening in the other person's life. The details are critically important, yet if we stay in this place our world has a funny way of getting smaller. Our viewpoint has a tendency of becoming limited because of the circumstances. However, this should be a cue for us conversationalists to move to the next level of significance. Will we remain conversationally limited or will we move to have our perspective broadened and open up our world to new possibilities? If so, we're moving to the next level.

Level #3: Conceptual Conversations— Potential Opportunities

Maybe we've just spent quite a bit of time wondering how we're feeling or responding to a specific situation. But what if that conversation moved to, "I wonder how that person was impacted by the situation? I wonder if that person would make the same decision if they had a little time of rest and the opportunity to sleep on their decision? I wonder what would happen if the leader had the opportunity to delegate that responsibility to somebody else who was more qualified?"

One of the most influential mentors in my life, Paul Stanley, often says, "We don't learn from experience; we learn from *evaluated* experience." Paul has taught hundreds of leaders what it is like to role-play scenarios rather than just responding when they happen. What if we were able to roll back the tape, replay the scenario—how would we have responded differently? Not only do we look at our response, but we also look at what we learn for the next time.

Could you imagine an organization that gave the grace and opportunity for people to make mistakes, come back, and evaluate, learn, and bring that learning in a spirit of humility, thus passing it along to fellow team members? Imagine a mentoring dialogue working through a difficult situation and how people would learn when that same mentor reminds them, "I remember when you went through this a few years back." The role of the conversation-alist investigates what's going on, analyzing different scenarios and possibilities that bring a fresh perspective. Conversationalists invite new concepts or ideas to be presented, such as, "Have you considered this possible scenario?"

Context is critically important for us to understand what is happening around us. Yet if we stay there for prolonged periods of time, it will potentially stifle our thinking and we'll become stuck in our own circumstances. Inviting fresh ideas is to facilitate brain-storming of new possibilities for a family. For example, "What do we want to do this weekend?" Or, "Where do we want to go on vacation?" Asking those questions could open up a number of new ideas from members in your family.

Conceptual is not all critical. It actually carries within itself the possibility to celebrate one another. If you have a person in your life, your family, or your team who has something significant to contribute, that is worthy of recognition—take the time to explore all of the different ways that person could be honored, valued, and truly celebrated for their accomplishments.

An organization and its leadership had a business model that had sustained them for over a decade, and yet one of their primary customers was renegotiating their contract and the likelihood that they would renew was not great. The organization's leader, who was so emotionally vested in this client after founding the business over a decade before, was almost too close to the scenario to think objectively. So, I did something I never had done before—I asked to have time with the organization's executive team offsite, without the leader attending.

My work for the team was to put together a series of business scenarios that would be presented in front of me and the team and be up for discussion. My role was to facilitate the brainstorming around each of these ideas, and by the end of the day we would have conceptually worked through a series of ideas and thus nar-rowed the focus, and then they would be presented back to the leader. That day was a blast for me—there were no politics, proto-cols, or procedures.

In the end, the organization's primary customer ultimately did phase out and almost a year to the date of the offsite meeting, the team launched a new business that leveraged the resources of their team, their past experiences, and strong relationships with their customers. At some point, the conversationalist identifies the problem that's going on or the challenge at hand and then takes that challenge and leverages it for the potential of future opportunities. Once these opportunities are defined, then it moves us to the next level of significance.

Level #4: Considerable Conversations— Discovering Priorities

The biblical inspiration of the conversationalist calls us to consider "how we may spur one another on toward love and good deeds" (Hebrews 10:24). When the concept of this book first hit the piece of scratch paper, it had the working title of *Considerable Conversations*. The truth is that every one of us are moved, spurred on, and motived in unique ways through considerable conversations. Casual is the introductory greeting to the relationship, contextual begins to define the problem at hand, and conceptual begins to open up the possibilities for what can happen. But considerable conversations narrow the focus to something that is deeply personal.

Another business advisor I often work with says, "The need does not determine the call." If we take time to consider all the conceptual opportunities that are presented to us, how can we possibly take advantage of them all? It is simply impossible. We have to narrow our focus for what we are going to do, and what we are going to do has to be aligned to what moves us deeply. For most people, as they grow in their responsibilities, their opportunities certainly grow alongside with them. Their need to be able to discern what is the best use of their time is critically important. Just because someone has a competency in an area doesn't necessarily mean that is what they should be doing for prolonged periods of time. It's a consideration but not necessary.

In his study on intrinsic motivation, Kenneth Thomas identified four areas of employee engagement that help build great culture and drive performance: meaningfulness, choice, use of competencies, and measureable progress. More than just extrinsic rewards (like salary and time off) and benefits (such as insurance and retirement planning), what moved organizations to higher levels of performance and a stronger culture was that their people actually were engaged with something that had an impact. In addition, they could contribute and speak into the process, which means they got to align their energies with their training and experience, having the opportunity to see and measure the results of their work. Such a study seems to agree with what would be common sense, but somehow we've lost it within most organizations, either because of bureaucracy, a drive for the bottom line, or a fear of too much independence.

Such conclusions provide us grounding points as conversationalists, so that we can engage with people by having considerable conversations. What if we used a set of criteria and evaluated our conversations? How many of our conversations throughout our week are mundane versus how many of them are meaningful? I don't have to probe too far with my teenage girls when talking about their school days sitting through classes—the conversations are boring and mundane. However, the conversations they experience when they go to their youth group at church are much different— they come home brimming with life because the conversations are so alive and dynamic and meaningful. These are considerable conversations because they get to the heart of what is most meaningful to us. These types of conversations unlock our passions, scratch on our purposes, and align our actions to priorities.

As a conversationalist, you can see the change and the energy represented in the countenance and the tone of voice of the other person when we have these types of conversations. This is because we have just hit on something that's considerable—more than a statement of grief, challenges at hand, or conceptual ideas that stimulate thinking. No, we've hit something that runs deep. As conversationalists, we need to be more than just entertained by someone else's energy; we need to explore what's actually going on. Why does this idea, this issue, or this individual represent such a deep charge of conviction?

When you can help people move through conversations of what matters most to them, you're moving into sacred space that is not often talked about or even explored. You're certainly not there for your own selfish gain; you're there to serve them by bringing light to areas in their life that may be shadowed or even confused. Why do they feel so deeply about this issue? When you can put words to things they feel so connected to but may have a difficult time expressing, you bring life to that person.

It is moving from implicit to explicit. If the conceptual asks the question of "what if" and explores the possibilities, then the considerable moves to why this is so important. Rarely when you ask the "why" questions are they so easily articulated. These are areas that need to be explored. As we're engaged with considerable conversations, this is ultimately the place of understanding. To explore is to navigate, and when you explore you're often in places you've never been before and you're not sure of where to go. You're dealing with the unknown.

Level #5: Catalytic Conversations— Defining Moments and Actions That Follow

When you summit a peak, you're rewarded with a view you may have possibly never seen before in your life. It's a perspective that nearly takes your breath away. It's that moment where your world enlarges, and somehow you know that you will never be the same again. Earlier this year, there was a youth conference in Colorado Springs that had thousands of teenagers from all over the country. We hosted several of the teenagers who are friends of our girls. At the end of the conference, I got to be the guide to take these teenage girls up to the summit Mount Princeton, one of the fifty-eight fourteeners in the Colorado Rocky Mountains..

One of the girls, who doesn't live in Colorado, had to face the realities of altitude. Another young girl just a few years before had struggled with an eating disorder that led her to the hospital. The fear of being too weak to do anything such as fourteener was overcome that day as these girls summited. When they arrived at the top, you could see the joy and the delight in their eyes. They had overcome their own fears and they had conquered, but they had done it with the encouragement of their friends along the way. These girls thought they could never do something like this, and yet there they were. The reality of being able to look out over that peak with a 360-degree changed view, the world from their eyes to their heart— they realized they could do something they thought was impossible.

As conversationalists, we're moving people into a place of encouragement in ways they have never experienced. And as we summit with them, in some ways our journey to the top invites us to be that encourager and advocate who helps facilitate through an inspirational moment. Inspirational moments are often experienced or categorized as we listen to a great message or watch something on a show that's reality based, yet what is different in a catalytic conversation is that we are talking about something that is not impersonal. We are not pulling off of somebody else's experience. This is something that we have deeply experienced for ourselves, and because of that, we are responding to it. That's what happened to these girls that day. Something shifted in them, from being able to summit a peak to being able to conquer internal fears they had never been able to overcome, and they did it with a community of other people.

The perspective on the mountain that day only illustrates a perspective that happens at the heart and mind level of those we converse with. These are moments of inspiration that say, "If I can conquer this mountain, what could I do that has been holding me back?" When a girl takes time to consider what matters most to her, she is working at a heart level she has not been able to fully articulate before. As the conversationalist, you get to be with that person at their moment of perspective and inspiration. You are there to be a witness to their moment, and you're in a position where you can celebrate, affirm, and encourage them.

The year 2011 was a season of a career transition and a lot of mountainside moments seeking clarity for my next steps. During that time, I discovered a personal mantra that really defines the work I do today in a coaching context: *moving leaders from inspiration to impact in their areas of influence.* It's a guiding statement for me as I often encounter people who are stuck. They're stuck in their own circumstances, paradigms, or perspectives because of their pain or their problems. When I can move people off their plateau and get them moving toward what matters most, there is not a greater point of satisfaction for me.

This is really the heart of catalytic conversations. We can have things that stir our hearts and that are considerable, but ultimately at what point do you take that step forward into your destiny? Even the word *destiny* is an overwhelming idea for most people. Destiny gives us an indication of our destination. When you've experienced that peak moment of inspiration, where your perspective has changed and you get a glimpse of what's ahead, then you are moving forward into that new reality.

In my work with leaders and teams, I conduct 360-degree interviews. One of the questions I ask within the interview is, "Within the next three years, where do you hope to see the leader and the organization?" The question always creates a pause, and it is fascinating listening to the answers of people who consider the possibilities. After hearing what they hope the future may hold, I'll often ask, "Where do you see yourself in that future? And what's your part to play to help that leader succeed?" Such questions reveal whether they believe in the leader, the organization, and its future. In addition, it reveals their commitment to its future. Oftentimes, such questions evoke emotion either in defense or a quiet and deep sincerity that's endearing and affirming to the leader.

In a recent interview, I was given a gift by listening to one of the team members who expressed, after working in the organization for nearly a decade, her need for a break. She dreamed of going abroad internationally and serving within a missions organization, only to return one day to serve within the organization better refreshed and with her world enlarged. Even in asking the questions, the dialogue gave her the clarity and the courage she needed to go and talk to her boss to set in motion a plan for her to live the next year of her life in a foreign context. This gave the organization the time it needed to shift her roles and responsibilities from within and hire the support they needed to cover her role.

I am fascinated by this story because it didn't take place during a mountainside moment, but rather the peak of her perspective came in a conference room over a 360-degree interview that focused on the leader. Within the course of an hour, we were talking about strategy, tactics, and even the dysfunctions of the organization. The catalytic conversation breaks the confusion, brings clarity, and follows with a confidence that scratches so closely to a person's calling, destiny, or his or her next destination.

As a conversationalist, you are potentially one conversation away from what may result in a life-inspiring change. This wasn't a new idea for this young lady; it was simply the first opportunity she had to truly express with clarity a dream that would lead to an action. And that's truly catalytic.

How many people are sitting right on the cusp of a decision that will have life impact for them, which will require courage for them to take action on, but also require courage for us as the conversationalist to press forward through the difficulty? Confusion and unknown, and the emotions that come with them, will often make us want to hit the eject button. Yet that's the moment we need to stay steady and sit within the unknown. More often than not in mentoring roles, we're a moment too quick to offer advice or solutions or to jump on new strategies or tactics for how to get there.

Whenever you're standing on that peak, it's so easy to see the next peak that you're ready to go explore. It's inspiring and motivating, and in that moment you have others surrounding you who are for you and believe in you—and you're ready to go conquer that next peak. Yet there're a few valleys to go through, a few rivers to cross, and trails to get you there. More often than not, our journey of life and our conversations that give words to our experiences are rare and beautiful moments where we need to simply enjoy and bask in the transcendence of the moment. When was the last time you were on that peak? Do you remember that feeling? It's a moment of joy, perspective, and peace that is hard to even put into words.

Getting Beyond the Demographic

One of my closest friends is a South African who's traveled the world the past twenty years as a missions pastor. He is one of the most brilliant strategic thinkers and has an understanding of worldview. This man spurs me on to love and good deeds just by being in his presence. Riaan would often counsel people that one has to get beyond the demographic. Certainly, that could be international; it could be national or out of your community or circles within your own bubble of relationships.

What's the demographic of your relationships? Who can you invite feedback from that will expand your worldview just by scheduling time at the local coffee shop? What dad or mom is doing a great job raising their kids who you could take to lunch and ask their perspective? What business leader is a little further along than you who could stimulate some fresh thinking from their models and competitive advantage? Who is a silver-haired person in your life who's lived faithfully and well, from whom you could seek advice, counsel, or even encouragement?

These are the considerable ideas that will spur you on toward love and good deeds, and by doing so they model the same for you to go and do likewise. As you look at these five levels of significant conversations, you may already operate well within all five of them. But even so, how can you be more intentional to engage people today?

As you move deeper within these levels of significance, you're moving closer to life-changing relationships. How do you get these conversations started? Where do you begin? What are the questions that will help to guide the discussions into further discovery? Let's step off the precipice and take the trail back down to the valley.

INSIGHTS AND ACTIONS

1. Who in life has engaged you in each circle? Write down their names.
2. Which circle do you spend most of your time in conversationally? Where are you the strongest, and where is the greatest need for growth?
3. Rank your skill and maturity in each circle from 1 to 10, with 1 being the weakest and 10 being the strongest.
   - Casual conversations—importance of the small things
   - Contextual conversations—perspective of the world around us
   - Conceptual conversations—potential opportunities
   - Considerable conversations—discovering priorities
   - Catalytic conversations—defining moments and actions that follow
4. What's one conversation you will have this week that will move you to the next level of intentionality?

Chapter 3

COMING TO THE TABLE

Growing up in Georgia, I was raised on good ole Southern hospitality. Driving up to Grandma's house for a Sunday afternoon dinner, I came expectant and hungry. As soon as she opened the door, standing there with her arms opened wide, my mouth was already watering with the smell of her culinary delights coming out of the kitchen. I know I am totally biased here, but she made the best sweet tea. She had the perfect glaze on that honey-baked ham. She would fry up some fatback for the perfect amount of flavor in the green beans. And she always had the right amount of cream for that creamed corn freshly pulled right from her garden.

Depending on the occasion, it was either cornbread in the cast iron pan hot out of the oven or homemade bread perfectly kneaded and risen that nearly floated away if it wasn't for the butter slathered on it. She would churn that ice cream to perfection after the meal, and she would make one of the lightest pound cakes you have ever tasted, layered with strawberries freshly cut from the vine. It's hard to even write about this without getting hungry. Grandma also spent time setting the table with the place settings laid out just right, glasses by each place, which made one feel like they were anticipated and welcomed into her home. Papa would be at one end of the table, and he would ask grace for the meal and we would dig in.

Grandma's table serves to represent childhood memories that have been burned and etched into my mind and heart, yet they also represent a thousand meals since and the conversations around those tables. As we progress in this book, it is important to think about conversations as a table you are setting in anticipation of relational fine dining. Just like the diversity of any menu, so it is with the conversations represented at each table. Regardless of your experiences with fine dining and leisure meals over many courses, most of us know the difference between a holiday celebration and fast food on the dollar menu.

We are living in a day and age where there's too much indulgence at the relational drive-through. In order for us to be great conversationalists who engage the heart of the listener and consider what spurs another on toward love and good deeds, we must first consider the table that we are setting for those conversations. Every table sets an atmosphere that lends itself for rich and meaningful conversations. The conversationalist proposes the idea that every conversation has the potential for a life-changing engagement. More than hype, quick fixes, or dollar-menu gimmicks, my hope is to cast a vision of the type of table you hope to conversationally set.

In the most traditional sense, the table represents a place in a home where family and friends gather to talk about life, school, work, the details of the day, and, when the occasion is right, hopes for the future. Grandma's table holds memories etched in my history, which conditions itself on the family conversations we have today at the dinner table.

Certainly, conversations are not limited to the dinner table alone. They can move into living rooms, to tables at the local coffee shop, among friends at the conference table within a work setting, or to a picnic table in the great outdoors. If you desire to grow in your relationships and your friendships with more meaningful engagements within your family, church, and workplace, one of the greatest ways to start is by setting the table.

Patterns, Programs, and People

Regardless of our backgrounds, each of us have models that have influenced how we engage in conversations. Whether you press in or hold back, whether you take time to reflect before responding or you are one of the "ready, fire, aim" kind of people—whether we like it or not, we are conditioned by both positive and negative models in our lives.

In our media-centric day, we are more influenced than we realize by movie icons, the celebrities on sitcoms we watch week after week, and the viral videos we see on social media. Just like a newborn with his parents, we imitate facial expressions, the tone of our voice, and even comments or humor. In no way are we carbon copies, because we are each our own unique person, finding our own unique expression; yet, regardless of our individuality, we still have a way of mimicking the models in our life for good or for bad.

For a conversationalist, the invitation is to look beyond family-of-origin issues that you may still be struggling with, mentors, bosses, friends, and other people of influence, and ask yourself, "What kind conversationalist do I want to be?" Being a conversationalist isn't about reconciliation, restoration, or even redemption, yet those ideas may find expression in the conversations we have. If you desire to grow in your ability to have life-changing relationships, then there has to be a place for forgiveness, healing, and peace over your past. Where you experienced great pain, once healed, it will lend itself for an even greater passion in your life.

When we talk about setting the conversational table, there are three ideas that are so basic they are often neglected. Yet these three ideas are key for setting the table for meaningful conversations: invitation, expectations, and preparation.

Invitation: Making It Personal

A few years ago a friend of mine from Atlanta was approaching his seventieth birthday and wanted to come out to Colorado for a day of skiing. Knowing that I had some knowledge of the slopes and that I love to ski, he reached out to discuss the possibility of some times to go skiing together. It was clear that he was going to be treating for the day, and my role was simply to host him and show him the slopes. He was a good friend of my father-in-law, so the day was coordinated where Bill, my father-in-law, would drive us up and Bob and I would hit the slopes. It was a perfectly sunny day for the drive, and the temperatures were almost perfect with the sunshine on our faces—a day meant for relaxing on the ski lift and adventuring wherever we could find the best powder.

I clearly remember the feeling I had that day—it was one of the best days of the year. I had over twenty years of history with this man, and during a short season of my young married years he was a mentor for me. It was a reunion of sorts, but in an adventurous kind of way. Through the conversation in the truck up and back, over greasy hamburgers at twelve thousand feet, and on and off the ski slopes throughout the day, I feasted conversationally with this old friend. Bob is a mentor, and I am marked by our relationship and his investment in my life. He modeled what it meant to be intentional.

Every conversation we have can range from scheduled to spontaneous, formal to informal, a prepared agenda to an open menu of questions that facilitate the time together. Whether you are inviting a friend to come and hang out or you're a proposing a major international trip, the invitation is your expression that says, "I value you. You are important enough to me and a priority in my life that I want to spend time with you." Most of us live our life out of routine and regularity, which can lose some of its creativity, spark, and enthusiasm at times if we are not intentional.

When my daughters, Ellie and Bethany, were young, they would dream about the theme of their party and which friends they wanted to be there, and then the expression of all that energy and creativity went into an invitation. Think about your relationships and who you are really wanting to connect with more in your life. Maybe it is someone you haven't seen in a long time, or someone you see regularly but don't get the chance to have meaningful conversations with. We run the risk that the most routine conversations may take for granted the people we care about most. Taking time to put a little creative energy into inviting people to something they value and even love to do is one of the greatest ways to add a spark back into our relationship. It is an invitation that lends itself for the possibility of fresh, insightful, and engaging conversations. A well-played invitation lends itself for great anticipation.

Expectations: Scheduling for Spontaneity and Planning for the Unexpected

Expectations can either be the framework to ignite life-changing conversations or shut them down because they are too structured. In this idea of conversationally setting the table, I personally struggle with the tension between leaving the agenda open and broad or putting too high expectations for what can actually be accomplished. I experience this in conferences and retreats on a more formal schedule, where we try to fit so much in that we will never accomplish, which creates its own frustration (or there's just not quite enough time, and we leave the table wondering what was really accomplished).

It's a real art to balancing a formal schedule, while leaving room for some spontaneity. You could argue that the clearer your expectations, the less likelihood of disappointment for your time together. Yet at the same time, if your conversation is *too* scheduled, then it has a tendency to feel stuffy and less personal. It is in this continuum between scheduled and spontaneous that I want to introduce a third idea—situational.

Just like in a good story, every conversation has the potential to take a turn because of the situation at hand. We see this all the time in family and friendships and even in business settings. Some new twist has happened that we were not expecting. Sometimes this can be exciting, because it presents new challenges to what our expectations were in our plans in the first place. It is important to be mindful of communicating appropriate levels of expectations that lend themselves for further relational development. But the opposite is true as well.

We all know what it is to step into relationships and the conversations they represent with a high level of expectations that are not met. Those disappointments have a way of deteriorating the health and strength of any relationship. As a general rule, the more complex the conversations, the greater the need to clarify the expectations beforehand. With the more informal conversations, you can still establish expectations even if you are just hanging out—yet if there is something happening in that person's life, you can send a quick text, letting them know you are looking forward to hearing more about their life.

Anticipation and expectations really do go hand in hand—clearer expectations prepare you for your time together. Expectation is heart preparation for a meaningful engagement, but it is also a discipline that we will unpack in more detail. Relationships live and die on expectations. What are you expecting when you come to the table? Once you have clarity on your own expectations, then you're ready to prepare the table.

Preparation of the Conversational Table

Holiday meals and birthday parties are rarely thrown together at the last minute. Certainly, there are aspects of our times together where we have creative whims, and it is those touches that make them really special. But more often than not, when we are hosting a party, Cari will set the dining room table a day or two in advance of our gathering: plates, glasses, silverware, flowers, candles, and in some cases she will actually take the time to put place cards with the people's names in front of the plate where they will be sitting. She does this often with great thought and consideration of the people who are coming, with the possibilities of conversations that may take place.

We host a lot of people in our home. If we are doing a larger gathering, it has more of an atmosphere of a party with burgers and chicken wings, and so it is not so formal to include place cards. Regardless of what's on the menu, I've seen it consistently over our twenty years of being married that when people walk into our home, the atmosphere is so inviting that they seem to be at ease the moment they walk through the door. As they take their jackets off and walk in through the foyer, and they get a smell of what's going on in the kitchen, I can see it on their faces—they can't wait to sit.

Whether you are hosting a conference, running a meeting within an organization, organizing a dinner group, or inviting a friend out for coffee, the little touches of preparation are almost always well received. Even in a one-on-one setting, when you take the time to pick up a book that goes into further depth about your friend's area of interest, it will be well received—especially if you gift the book to your friend as well. But more importantly, taking an interest lends itself to the possibility of going conversationally deeper than you may have ever done before.

The idea of preparation has everything to do with getting ready. More than gifts, place settings, or meal preparations, what has the potential and the greatest impact is the preparation of your heart for the conversation. Taking time to consider what is happening in that person's life and thinking through the questions to help draw him or her out is valuable. It certainly could be a big theme of what's happening in a particular season of that person's life or it could be paying attention to the smallest details of a little passing comment.

Conversationally setting the table has more to do with your own heart, which conditions your attitude and sets people at ease, letting them know you really care and are sincerely interested in what's going on in their world. As we build on this idea of what's happening at the table of conversation, the greatest things we can often do for the conversation happen before we are even having the conversation itself.

What's Experienced at the Table

Now that we are at the table of conversation and the preparations have been made, we are ready to sit and engage. But what happens at the table? What do people experience? How you communicate, how you ask questions, and how you engage with the people in your life adds to the potential of enriching their lives and yours. Yet what moves us are the specific people in our lives, so look at your family relationships, friendships, and a few key people in your life. As you consider for yourself the table you are wanting to conversationally set, think in terms of specific people you would like to take these ideas and put them to work to help build meaningful and life-engaging relationships. It is often not what's communicated in those exchanges that is the most important but more often what people feel and experience after being with you.

There are three ideas of what is experienced at the table. Whether I am looking at my grandmother's table growing up, mentoring conversations with people who have had an impact on my life, or other moments that are life-defining experiences, I reflect and consider what was happening in those moments that made them so unforgettable. As you look at your own life, whether those experiences have been many or few, I would suggest that there are some common themes you can observe, learn from, and bring into the conversations and the table you are setting today. These three experiences are: to be loved, listened to, and led.

To Be Loved

To consider "how we may spur one another on toward love and good deeds" (Hebrews 10:24) suggests the possibility that the greater the love and consideration you have directly impacts how much spurring will result. The greater you love the person you're spending time with, the greater the consideration should be because you care deeply for him or her. To love and to be loved is really the foundation for the conversationalist. Your ability to receive love and to give that love away has everything to do with your effectiveness as a conversationalist who is able to build deep relationships.

As you look at the people in your life and how you legitimately, genuinely, and sincerely care for them, I hope and pray that you can think of at least one person in your life who has sincerely, unashamedly, with all their heart loved you. It is because of that love relationship you have been given a capacity to love other people well. As we look at the models in our lives, it's worthy to reflect on those models that have simply loved us well. It isn't as much about the well-crafted questions as much as it is about the spirit of the relationship in which they are asked.

> To love and to be loved is really the foundation for the conversationalist.

The greatest impact you can have conversationally is to be able to love people in a way that is truly selfless, with a heart to serve rather than to be served. Certainly, in this area of love we have to contextualize based on the appropriate level of the relationship and given the priorities in our life and those whom we already have commitments to, such as our families and other closer relationships. We are talking about loving the world by loving our neighbor. But there are appropriate levels that can be difficult to articulate. Even Jesus himself went from town to town with a healing power to have impact in people's lives, yet he was selective about who he spent time with. There certainly is a level of discernment that is needed.

Love is the foundation for any relationship, and if we want to move further into those relationships it has to start with an authentic love for that person. When we talk about how we hope people experience those moments with us conversationally, it can have a variety of expressions. Let me start here: to love people well is ultimately to value them. After a few minutes of conversation, even if it is for the first time, people feel valued because of your time spent with them. Even in the look in your eyes and the countenance of your face, they can tell you sincerely care, and they feel delighted in.

Delight suggests that in a world that carries burdens, concerns, and worries, there is something in your manner where, even in the midst of such difficulties, there is a lightness about who you are. And you bring that lightness and celebrate it by speaking it out. It could be through listening to a story and repeating certain details that can be extraordinary, or it can be by taking that extra time to speak a word of affirmation. It is almost as if there is a sparkle in your eye when you are listening to the details of their life. Your language in response to their comments or story can spark them in a way that is so rare simply because you delighted in them and they felt it. You enjoyed them.

We hopefully know what it feels like to be with somebody who simply enjoys our company and being together, not because of what was said or done, but because their mere presence invokes a joy that wasn't there before. I am reminded of several occasions of long road trips where I spent hours in the car with Cari and the kids. As we traveled, we shared stories or laughed or sang to music, but for the most part it was quiet as we had plenty of windshield time. Often those are some of the best moments because one enjoys being with somebody without having to be "on" all the time.

There are so many moments in the course of our year that could be celebrated. Oftentimes, we fail to do so because of busyness, forgetfulness, or neglect. Great conversationalists will pay attention to such moments and simply acknowledge them in appropriate ways, whether it's in a private or a public setting.

To love people well, the language of our conversations that give expression to that love in appropriate ways has the potential for people to feel valued, delighted in, enjoyed, and celebrated, yet these are responses that we cannot manufacture. Hopefully, these are emotions people experience as a result of being with us. They are the expressions of what you have felt having been loved well by a few people in your own life. We want to move this forward into our conversations so that when we love well it lends itself to the possibility of life-changing implications—even in the simple fact that some people have never been loved at this level.

To love well is the foundation for the conversationalist. We have been discussing ways to have better conversations, questions that draw people out, and the disciplines that will help make us better conversationalists. But in the absence of love, it will all be ineffective. Let me illustrate this.

Well into my grandfather's eighties, he experienced something that represents being loved well. In his adult life, he experienced some significant disappointments that came through relationships, his vocational work, and in his own health, so that some people experienced him as the stereotypical grumpy old man. There were moments where he acted much like Archie Bunker in the old '70s sit-com *All in the Family*. I tend to remember him more like the Disney movie *Up*, where there are pieces to his story that were simple and wholesome, yet the ache of life not turning out like he had hoped left him feeling somewhat alone in life. And then a knock on his door from a little Boy Scout named Russell changed his world.

In the same way, my grandfather started coming to church with us early in his eighties. Somehow, a small group of retired and senior folks adopted my grandfather and celebrated his age and wisdom to the point where they gave him his own parking spot at church with his name on a sign. In addition to that, this was during the time that my girls were born and the mere presence of two little girls that were bouncing on Great-Grandpa's knee transformed this man. Those who knew him watched a transformation from a stern (and at times angry) man to a grandfatherly type who had a contagious smile on his face. I saw my grandfather finish well in life because he was loved well and passed that love onto other people.

To Be Listened To

One of the greatest ways you can honor people is by taking time to listen to them. As illustrated at the beginning of the chapter, the difference between a Thanksgiving meal at Grandma's versus fast food from the dollar menu is how well we listen conversationally. Before we get into what kind of questions we should be asking, we must first explore an attitude and a spirit of curiosity that represents some level of fascination about another's life.

Curiosity engages the listener. Some of those details really do matter. So often the temptation is to judge the book by its cover, and we stereotype too quickly and miss out on the wealth of the potential of a meaningful relationship. When people experience you as curious about their life, it seems as if people are almost skeptical of your curiosity because it is such a rare experience today. Rarely do people ask questions beyond the trivial. As we listen better and people experience our sincerity, we move from curiosity to learning more about their lives.

When we consider what spurs someone on toward love and good deeds, we are moved for more reasons than, we have to or we are supposed to do something. We are spurred on because there is something that is a high priority at a heart level—and even a purpose for our life. If we are drawing on that deep well of knowledge, we are listening intently to learn more about what matters most in people's lives. As we move conversationally by listening, we discover that the closer something is to the heart, the more it reveals why something is so important to someone. More often than not, that "why" is a significant part of their story. So as we engage as a listener, we are moving to a place that has a level of significance and that moves us to the possibilities of sympathy as we listen to the stories of their life.

> When we can engage conversationally and relate at a level of common interest, it creates a bond that strengthens the foundation of relationships that future conversations will be built upon.

When we can engage conversationally and relate at a level of common interest, it creates a bond that strengthens the foundation of relationships that future conversations will be built upon. These are rare gifts and experiences that seem so simple, and yet they are so rarely experienced today. But what creates the possibility of the third element of what someone can experience conversationally?

To Be Led

I remember it like it was yesterday. We were sitting at that same table just after finishing a Christmas meal. My aunt and uncle were in town from Montana, and I, as a twelve-year-old boy, without any prompting, grabbed the dishes off the table and went into the kitchen to wash them (I am rather proud of myself as I write this now). What made that moment so memorable to me was that after I finished the dishes, my grandma came up and gave me a silver dollar. This was more than just a regular dollar one would get for doing chores—this was a *silver* dollar she held in safekeeping and was a special acknowledgement for a voluntary act of an adolescent boy.

In addition to the money being given, I also remember my aunt and uncle talking about me over dessert, saying, "I think Russell is ready to come to camp." It was an acknowledgement of a maturity and readiness. There was something in the statement that said they believed in me, which was represented in an invitation to come up to Montana to their Christian camp.

As a thirteen-year-old, I would get on a plane and fly from Georgia to Billings, Montana, and then there would be a five-hour drive out to eastern Montana. That adventure defined my faith, my teenage years, and my coming into manhood. One moment over a holiday meal and the conversations that happened before and after—I am still talking about them all these years later. The conversations that you have possess the potential for life-changing implications, not only for how well you love people and how well you listen to them but also for how the conversation leads them.

Future. When you move conversationally to talk about someone's future, you open up a whole dimension for the way people think. You're not just focusing on past issues or present challenges, but about future possibilities that don't yet exist. In addition, when you are in those conversations, there is a connection for the potential of those opportunities, and the one asking is proposing that he or she wants to be part of that future.

The most intimate form of communication is when you are at a point of talking about your dreams and your fears. When you are talking conversationally about the future, it's the ultimate invitation of where you see yourself and how someone can walk alongside you into that future. I remember such a moment with clarity—sitting in a corner booth at an IHOP, having pancakes and terrible coffee, with a friend of mine who was dreaming about a business he hoped to create one day. He had a dream to be able to give away $1 million a year for love and good deeds.

We were in a considerable conversation of what it would take to spur him on to create an enterprise that would generate that kind of income to see that dream fulfilled. Some fifteen years later, my friend is still working toward that dream, but the impact of his life is extraordinary, whether or not he gives away a $1 million a year. The joy for me was that I got to be a witness to such a dream some fifteen years ago and see the expression of it in his life today.

Change. Change can be one of the most daunting things any of us have ever faced. That role of a mentor who's been a little further along the path can often lead us conversationally to where we are going and also help define what changes need to take place in our lives, giving us a sense of clarity to do something that we have never done before.

Challenge. Every change in our life represents potential new challenges. Spurring one another on toward love and good deeds doesn't exactly evoke images of Pollyanna, fairy tales, or cute clichés to move us forward. Spurring can be hard. Proverbs 27:17 declares, "As iron sharpens iron, so one person sharpens another." If you aspire to do great things, then you are likely going to face great challenges in your life. A conversationalist can walk alongside of you amid those challenges, spurring you in ways to help keep your focus where it needs to be. The greatest temptation when we face challenges is to lose heart and possibly even lose our way.

Guide. Conversationalists help lead us, remind us, and encourage us on the path that's before us, helping us to not get off track, distracted, or discouraged. They act as a guide. When you are facing the unknown, moving into places you've never been can be daunting. It is still your trek and your journey, yet a guide who helps point you in the right direction imparts a confidence that you might not be able to muster up on your own. Such a guide may not necessarily have all the answers, but maybe they have traveled that road before and can provide you some key points that are critical for where you are headed.

When we went to Africa, my friend Tim, who was the one who invited us and hosted our trip, was taking us to places he had been before, which gave him a confidence for what our experience was going to be like. But he had never taken his son on an adventure like that. In addition, we were going to other places in Africa where he had never been, and he was relying on his guide when we came to those areas. Ultimately, the role of the guide takes us to places we could never get to on our own.

Model for the Future: Where Are You Headed?

I have invited you to look at the table that has been set for most of your life, to look at the table that has influenced you, and how you set the conversational table for the relationships in your life today. My hope is that you have been spurred on with new possibilities through the place settings of engaging the people in your life, with an intentionality of how you invite, and the anticipation of your time together. This comes by clarifying the expectations and what you can do to prepare for a meaningful moment that has life-changing possibilities. We've looked at what people experience in the most memorable moments in our lives and realized that we can glean from these experiences today, bringing them forward into our conversations by loving people well, listening to the stories of their lives, and then leading the conversations into moving forward.

Such models and moments can influence you, but they do not have to define you. You have an opportunity today to conversationally start bringing these ideas forward into your relationships. As you do this, it prepares your heart as well as those you are engaging with for conversations unlike what you have ever experienced before.

Where are you conversationally headed? What kind of conversationalist do you hope to become? As you look at your life today, are you experiencing most of your relationships from the fast food lane? How often do you experience the richness of a holiday meal with the people you care most about?

We are moving from the table of conversation to engaging at the next level, which is discernment. What's going on with this person and how can I help? What's my part to play in their story? We are at the heart of the conversationalist, discerning what is often not on the surface yet is present in everyone's life. We are discerning what everyone longs for but few receive.

INSIGHTS AND ACTIONS

1. What have been the most defining conversations in your life?
2. Commit to engage one of your most important relationships this week. Which way will you be intentional in engaging with them?
   a. Send them a meaningful invitation.
   b. Clarify your expectations for your time together.
   c. Prepare to make the most of the meeting.
3. After you intentionally engage with them, evaluate how it went with your conversationalist partner.
   a. Did they feel valued?
   b. Did they feel listened to?
   c. Did they leave with the opportunity for future conversations?

Chapter 4

WHAT EVERYONE LONGS FOR
BUT FEW RECEIVE

It was three in the morning, and I was trying to sleep but not doing a very good job of it. I was tossing and turning, struggling with my jetlag when the phone rang. The guy in the bunk next to me answered the phone and said, "Hey, what's going on?" Over the next few minutes, Dave began asking a series of questions, engaging in a coaching conversation, as I was trying to put the pillow over my head so I could sleep. When most people were trying to sleep, including me, Dave was modeling what it means to engage in a meaningful coaching conversation even at the most bizarre hour.

We were outside of Oslo, Norway, in a little farming community on a snowy countryside in a farm house. That was to be our quarters for the next five days. Our hosts, Gunter and his wife, had been with Youth With A Mission for almost forty years. They were Germans who moved to be missionaries in South Africa, and later Gunter completed his PhD at Oxford. He had invited my friend and mentor, Paul, to come with a group of men to have some conversations on holiness. Gunter had been a student on the subject for most of his life, particularly the last ten years.

I had traveled the world. I'd been on mission trips and certainly attended my share of conferences, but I had never been invited to come to the other side of the world for the purpose of having conversations around a subject with a small group of spiritual leaders. I was young guy in my late thirties, while the other five guys were in their late fifties and sixties, with one guy in his seventies.

What everyone longs for but few receive is something that is soul-deep, something that few even realize until they get a taste of it. Going to the other side of the world with the anticipation and expectation to have conversations around a subject I barely felt like a novice in seemed like a stretch. I was secure in who I was, yet there were moments where I felt like the schoolboy coming into the classroom I had no business being in. At the same time, I was getting ready to be schooled in far more than just an intellectual exercise on the subject of holiness. It's more than just knowing—it's something that's experienced. And it's through those experiences that each of us are shaped.

The Gift of Story

Over the course of that trip, I engaged in, but more so experienced, conversations that shaped my thinking. As wonderful and engaging as the lessons taught by the professor were, more impactful was my individual time with the men. When you're in that level of proximity, sharing your thoughts at that level, there is an exchange that happens that creates a bond in relationships that marks you for a lifetime.

After Dave finished his call with his nephew, something about his manner and the specifics of his questions were so intriguing to me in my half-stupor that I turned on the bedside lamp. I propped up my pillow, wanting to talk for a few minutes, which led into the early hours before sunrise. Dave guided me through a conversation that unlocked my story to a deeper level than I had before. I knew Dave was a safe place, that he believed in me, and that he could help me. So I laid down any inhibitions and relaxed into answering his questions. This exchange unlocked places in my heart that were life-giving and life-defining, where Dave modeled what it was to be a conversationalist. What everyone longs for but what few receive is knowing and being known.

What moves us further into these life-giving relationships, and the moments that define them, is someone of discernment who can help guide the conversation to such places. Those people help unlock our story and the things that matter most to us. What was modeled for me in Norway is that if we take the time to intently listen, then we can skillfully guide the conversation. This is because the story causes the questions to rise to the surface: "The purposes of a person's heart are deep waters, but one who has insight draws them out" (Proverbs 20:5).

As conversationalists, we need to be able to discern the questions that help unlock the heart. Each of the ideas presented here are important, yet the ideas of conversational discernment may be the most important principles for any individual wanting to engage in deeper levels of relationships. The lack of discernment is one of the fastest ways to cut off relationships. If you want to move forward in your relationships, then you have to understand and discern what the person needs so you are able to serve them better.

Conversational Comparisons: Dangers of the Careless and the Clueless

One of the fastest ways to shut down relationships is coming in with your own agenda and using relationships for the ultimate purpose of self-serving rather than serving the needs of those you are in dialogue with. We all know that feeling of being with somebody who lacks such discernment. I was recently introduced to a leader who runs a publically traded company. He had some expressed interest in learning about the work I do with CEOs and wanted to get together, so through e-mail exchange and texts, we finally did connect over lunch.

As we sat down for lunch, this high-energy, charismatic leader engaged with a few pointed questions to learn about me and about my executive coaching and consulting work, and I shared a little about my background. With a few skillfully crafted questions, he was able to glean from me some key points of information that he would artfully weave back into his presentation over the next forty-five minutes. During that time together, he waxed eloquent over his family, his work, his church involvement, his community commitment, businesses he had started and sold, orphans who had been fed, city governments that had been influenced, and books that had been written. At first I was intrigued, even entertained, and then something began to turn the conversation.

Within the course of a few minutes, he would move from quoting business trends from *Fortune* magazine to statistics in the stock market to poetry, and then name-drop famous celebrity pastors, quoting messages that had been given. Then he would weave back the conversation to societal impacts on cultural trends today and how political leaders he was friends with were making decisions because of his counsel. Since I am a conversationalist, I have experience guiding conversations, even when I felt like I couldn't get a word in edgewise. Since it was our first meeting, and since so many people had said we should get together, I was patiently waiting for the reason of our connection.

What started with a few questions that were pointed in my direction seemed to be the excuse which allowed him to eat his lunch and to give him some conversational preparations to dominate our time together. It concluded with him making a pitch for me and people in my network to invest in his company. His interest in me and in my work seemed to be only as good as what I could do for him, despite his elegance, sophistication, intellect, impressive performance and background—economically, socially, and apparently spiritually. I couldn't wait to get out of that lunch. I felt used, misunderstood, and misrepresented. I left feeling like I had been assaulted, nearly vomited on with his agenda. He is perhaps one of the most narcissistic men I have ever witnessed in conversation.

If we take a moment to reflect, most of us have experienced people like this. They are conversations with the careless and the clueless. They are careless in the sense that as I share even a remote story, that story has not been received as a point of caring for who I am, but was rather used as leverage to build his presentation to me. He's clueless in the sense that he has no idea of the wake he has left, where I am barely able to engage, respond, or even relate. It is clear that he was really there to be impressed with himself. And whatever I have done, whether great or little, is no match to what he had done; therefore, he left the lunch feeling better about himself.

We all have some level of insecurity when we approach relationships. However, one of the greatest ways to settle insecurities is by serving rather than being served. Working at the heart of the conversation is critical when we look at discernment, because if you were there entering into conversations with a motivation that is self-serving, then your discernment is going to be clouded. Ultimately, the heart of the conversationalist is to look at the people in your life and those you are engaging in conversations, then ask the question, "What do they need?"

Considering the needs of others above the needs of yourself is the line of maturity that sets the table and prepares the relationships for the possibility of a life-changing moment. This sounds like such a simple idea, but the reality is that it is a rare experience to interact with people who have a heart posture of complete selflessness and who engage in conversations that are free of an agenda. As conversationalists, we need to discern what's going on in the world of these people.

The idea of discerning the needs of others can be overwhelming at times. The needs of our own lives are often overwhelming, let alone trying to truly probe into the lives of other people. Your responsibility as a conversationalist is not to solve people's problems. Many times people are in situations that are absolutely out of their control and they are responding to them, whether it's in their family life, their friendships, or in their workplace. They may be facing circumstances they have absolutely no influence over, and yet they are trying to respond the best they can given the time and resources they have available.

However, many people are dealing with issues within their control. Many times they have not had the opportunity to have somebody who is safe, who believes in them, and who can truly help them. Remember that help is not solving their problem; a conversationalist guides them through a discussion to their own discovery that brings clarity. When they are on that path of discovery, where they can see and discern the impact of their own decisions, they take another level of responsibility for those decisions. As a conversationalist, you can be a champion for those decisions as people move forward. Your role is not writing the check to pay for their solution; the greater gift is helping them discern and then navigating the next steps.

Conversational Discernment: What Do They Need?

The criteria for the conversationalist to discern what people need falls into three categories: care, counsel, and courage. Working with these ideas for a number of years now, I have been testing them in friendships, coaching sessions, and team engagements. These three points are not exhaustive in any way, but they are a helpful set of grounding points that, as you are working through conversations and listening to the needs of people, allow you to know how to respond and engage with them. As you look at each of these three areas of care, counsel, and courage, depending on your personality, background, and unique experiences, you will recognize that you have a strength, a stretch, and a struggle operating within each one.

For example, I can smell fear a mile away from a person who is right on the cusp of a decision and needs to have breakthrough and the courage to be able to step across that threshold into their new reality. To speak courage into them is where I thrive, but you could look at any of my personality assessments and ask anyone who had known me for very long and find out that I am not high on mercy. It's not that I don't care; it's just not my strongest trait.

By comparison, Debbie, my sister-in-law and a labor and delivery nurse, is off the charts in the area of care and nurture. Not only do we need to discern what is going on conversationally with the needs of those people whom we are interacting with, but as we go through this we need to consider our areas of strength, stretch, and struggle in how we operate with people. Let's unpack these keys to discernment.

Care

Who nurtures the relationship? If you were to take the three areas of discernment and break them into three questions, then care is the "who." When you can ask who is the most impacted by this situation, more often than not it's the person who's sharing their concern. It seems so obvious because the situation demands a level of care. If a person has fallen down and is struggling to rise again, our role as caregiver is to simply pick them up, dust them off, and get them on their way.

The old adage that people don't care how much you know until they know how much you care is true. It's so obvious when we see a situation and we move to immediately solving the problem and offering a solution. Earlier this week, I had the opportunity for a brief five-minute conversation with a man who looked exhausted, as he had recently moved to town with his family. He was a firefighter who was out of work and looking for a job in construction in the meantime. He was at a point where he wasn't getting enough income to meet his financial needs, so he was experiencing some disappointment. In a brief exchange while waiting for his family, where I knew we only had a few minutes and there wasn't time to get into the details, I listened to his story. Some of his story resonated with mine, so I was able to look him sincerely in the eye and say, "Brother, I've been there, and I know it is hard. I know you're going to make it. Let me know how I can help." I don't know the impact that statement had, but taking the time to listen to him is what this man needed in that moment. When I asked if he had some people in his life who could walk beside him, he told me he only had to ask. My role in that moment was to listen and provide care.

My temptation is to always help solve the problem, yet solving problems is not the priority when one needs to stop and catch one's breath. When we conversationalists ask how somebody is doing and what we can do to help, just the act of listening to their answer sometimes does more than we can possibly imagine. More often than not, there are people who may have never expressed the full weight of what they are dealing with, and just speaking it out causes them to realize it is time to respond because they have been carrying a burden for which they need resources beyond their own abilities. Don't fix. Just listen and let them process.

A CEO friend of mine took his wife on a mission trip some time ago. It was their first time as a married couple that they had gone to Africa to work in an orphanage. The combination of the poverty and the needs of the children, as well as the new surroundings, was a shock to their marriage. The physical and emotional drain was exhausting to his wife. And, as we all well know, when we are exhausted we often say things we don't mean. In addition, when exhausted we hear things that cause a greater level of hurt than what was intended. As my friend would share after the trip, the greatest temptation for him in that moment was to offer solutions, tying to minimize the stress. Yet better judgment prevailed, and rather than trying to fix, he listened and acknowledged her stress, her own grief for seeing people struggling. Rather than issuing judgment, they just stood their ground and let grace and love prevail in the midst of a difficult situation.

So often when we see people experience stress, we want to provide solutions. This element of care seems obvious when people are in pain, but it's amazing how we lack discernment and offer solutions and prescriptive statements, instead of simply standing with somebody in the midst of their need. Far too many relationships have been divided during moments of tragedy and deep disappointment with canned statements that seem to trivialize the present difficulty. Life is messy sometimes. We've all been in these situations, either by experiencing them ourselves or just by witnessing them. One of the greatest acts of discernment is to acknowledge when you are hurting and choose not to extend that hurt to those around you.

For us to understand the anxiety, worry, or fear that we are experiencing, we need to take the time we need to recover, rest, and regain our perspective. The role of discernment and seeing where care is needed ultimately is to nurture the relationship. If you're at a point where you are no longer able to see objectively, to provide nurture because you need nurture, then you need to take a step back until you're healthy enough to re-engage. Before counsel, care comes first.

Before counsel, care comes first.

What everyone longs for yet few receive comes by knowing and being known. Taking the time to listen to another's story provides a care that allows the details to unlock your deepest values, priorities, and pains, which, once healed, are actually transformed into areas of passion and compassion. Trying to discern the significance of why things happen in a moment can be nearly impossible because we lose a level of objectivity. Compare this with taking time as a conversationalist to ask meaningful questions that unlock what people were feeling during those times, thus acknowledging the difficulty or success of that season. Maybe one of the greatest ways you can serve another is by asking meaningful questions around what they are presently experiencing.

Think for a moment of those people in your life who, whenever you've faced difficulties, have come alongside you and cared for you. Think of those people as models—not so much what was said in the moment but how they made you feel, which somehow transferred a quiet confidence that allowed you to catch your breath and pick yourself back up. You were then able to move forward and to respond in a healthy, life-giving way. Somewhere along the way we sense that person has caught their breath and they're ready to move forward, and thus the questions shift from care to counsel.

Counsel

As you cross the state line from any direction in Colorado, you will see the sign, "COLORADO, Land of Many Colors." And it's certainly true to its name. From the red rocks of Garden of the Gods to the golden aspens to the snowcapped mountains of Summit County, the fifty-three fourteeners offer a peak perspective. Throughout this state of many colors, there are shallow streams to mighty waters of the Arkansas River and the Colorado River. These waters are home to world-renowned fly fishing streams that bring anglers in from all over the world. I am no expert fisherman, but I have had my experiences catching fish in these waters and the many conversations around them.

As we talk about discernment, I want to draw three parallels that are essential to being a good fly fisherman. First, the glasses themselves. Coming to the water's edge with your natural eye, it is nearly impossible to see with the glare and reflection on the water. You have to have a pair of polarized glasses that minimize the glare and allow you to see into the water, and even then you still struggle to see the fish. But the key to becoming a good fly fisherman is seeing where the fish are.

Second, as a fly fisherman, you have to know what's biting. Whether you go to an expensive fly shop and look at all the pretty colors, buy some online, or make them by your own hand—no matter how pretty they are or how closely they resemble the insects on the water, if that doesn't appeal to the appetite of the fish in that given moment, then you are wasting your time. In addition to having the fly, you'll often use a double lead. The downside of such a technique is that it is easily snagged, but it creates a double possibility of catching your fish. In theory, as the first fly goes by it tempts and teases the fish, and then the fish may actually go for the second fly.

The glasses represent knocking down the glare and distraction of what's happening on the surface, allowing you to see what's going on underneath, it's the discernment we need to see what's truly going on. The flies themselves represent the questions we are asking. We all know the experience of asking questions that don't really catch, yet it may be the second question that creates a hook. Or, like all good anglers, if they're not getting a bite, they will pull their line and change their fly to something that may be more attractive.

Third is the question of water flow. You can have all the right gear and all the right flies, but if you go out in springtime or right after a rain, you'll never catch anything. The volume of water is so much that you can't see the fish because the waters are so muddy, not to mention the fact that the fish aren't biting compared to when the waters are clear and flowing normally. As an angler, I have personal experience with times of catching fish, but I've also had times where I've gone and caught absolutely nothing at all—it feels like a complete waste of time.

If you've ever had those moments where you feel like you're asking questions that aren't getting any bites, then these three points may help your ability to discern what is happening in that person's life below the surface. What are the right questions that are going to engage more meaningful dialogue? Understanding the pace of life in which you're casting the questions is important here—do they even have the time, energy, or capacity to respond in a meaningful way?

The conversationalist proposes seven life-changing questions that, if you actually take the time and have the courage to engage in them, have the potential to inspire, challenge, and be the catalyst for a real difference in a person's life. The first step in making such a difference begins with discernment. The true art of the fly fisherman is a natural rhythm that gracefully lays the line on the water with the potential of a great catch. Those with less grace and skill often tangle their line before it even hits the water or rifle the line across the water in such a way that it scares the fish. For the fly fisherman, it's all about the presentation, which is much the same for the conversationalist.

Readiness. Proverbs clearly shares with us that with a multitude of counselors plans will succeed (Proverbs 15:22). When we face challenges, we absolutely need to receive counsel. Trying to act independently quickly gets us into trouble, either because we have overexhausted ourselves or we have overextended our ability to see and have a healthy perspective. When we bring counsel into an issue, however, it puts a different lens on the treasure we seek. As we go from having a single point of counsel to multiple points, it allows us to see the issue from many different perspectives, thereby minimizing our blind spots. Having a multitude of counselors certainly does not eliminate the risk, although it does minimize it.

As a conversationalist, the most valuable counsel you can give is not so much in the answers you provide but in the questions that are asked. The seeking of wise counsel can be facilitated in informal settings as well as formal. The more complicated the issue or challenge, the more formal or disciplined you should be in your pursuit of understanding. More than the counsel itself is the willingness of the person seeking the counsel to acknowledge that they need help and are willing to receive some feedback.

As an executive coach, I will often ask when meeting with someone for the first time if they have ever been coached before. Many people have not and, no criticism implied, there's a certain level of readiness and assertiveness to receive feedback in the form of questions. Some of these questions may have never been asked before. The temptation for any of us would be defensiveness. Once somebody crosses the threshold, they are ready to receive the advice they seek.

Counsel is tricky because when we are seeking outside feedback, we often have a tendency to go where we can hear what we want to hear (i.e., the therapist's office, the kind of attorney we're looking for, or even the doctor's office). But when we are seeking outside help, we often go to friendships that may have a tendency to empathize with what we are going through, without necessarily providing a different perspective than what we want to hear. When we seek counsel only to have validation of what we are already planning to do, we somewhat defeat the purpose of seeking advice in the first place. The greatest counsel is often from the perspective of those who think differently than we do. We are not looking for a group of antagonists for the sake of it, but we are creating a tension of perspectives that don't see the same situation through the same pair of glasses. We need different viewpoints from different angles and shades so we can have a fuller picture of what's going on. When we have an issue that comes up, who is the counsel we keep? Do we have a tendency to hear what we want to hear, or do we invite feedback from a multitude of counselors?

Teachability. If the first level of discernment and counsel is readiness, then the second would be teachability. As a Christian in my teenage years, I was exposed to some teaching in the Navigators and by its founder, Dawson Trotman. In helping to discern who they wanted to work with, they used to work from an acronym—FAT, which stood for *faithful, available,* and *teachable.* As an organization that is focused mostly on collegiate students, how do you discern who to work with? Such an acronym gave them criteria for their leadership and who they wanted to invest their time in. As I think about working with people as a conversationalist, I realize there must be an openness to new ideas and thinking as well as differing perspectives.

If you are working with somebody who is set in their ways, then it can be a challenge when presenting new ideas or fresh perspectives. Another way to present this issue of teachability is from a principle that leaders are learners. Your circles of influence reflect your leadership, whether it's in the workplace, home, or church. The effectiveness of your influence has everything to do with what you are learning and how you are applying that learning to your leadership.

As you begin to understand what is happening in the person's life and their need for counsel, one way to begin unlocking the counsel they need is by listening to the questions they are asking. It's a simple idea, but it forces another level of thinking into the situation. Once a question is asked, it reveals their level of thinking and openness to new ideas.

When you talk with someone, you simply ask them about the counsel they need, and if it is followed up with a presentation filled with lots of details that comes across airtight, then you know there is no real room to speak into it. This gives you the discernment you need about how teachable and ready that particular person is to learn, which gives you a good indication of your openness to speak into or ask the heart-level questions. Each question actually draws us nearer and helps the conversation move with a greater level of focus and clarity.

Clarity. Consider for a moment the most significant issues you have faced in the last year. These are either opportunities or challenges that have stretched you, your team, and maybe even your family to the point where you need fresh insight and discernment. The more complex the issue, the more often there is a cloud of confusion and a fog of frustration surrounding that issue. When we're in that place of not being sure which way to go, the next step to take, or how to respond, one of the most liberating things is to have fresh insight.

A well-crafted question or series of questions can bring much-needed clarity to complex situations. Like shedding light on a little bit of darkness, it opens up thinking and brings a level of objectivity to what otherwise could be filled with a lot of emotion. In addition to seeking clarity, it often allows you to identify points of tension, which in turn allows you to evaluate where there are levels of risk or where faith needs to be applied. This is critical because it allows you to understand the areas within your control and the areas outside of your control. In doing so, you identify the resources you need in order to meet those challenges.

When you get clarity over complex issues, it gives you a track on which you can turn. Counsel is like the guardrails on a highway, which allow you to move farther and faster with a greater level of focus. Without such clarity and counsel, it leaves you dabbling and moving around, only experimenting with things, which, at times, is necessary, but which can be exhausting when you are on your own, putting your energies in the areas that may not be best. Counsel reminds us of what is important and why it's important, as well as how we are to apply ourselves. When we are finally at a point where the relationship has been nurtured and clarity has been achieved through a collective counsel, then we are at a point of decision. And it is at this point where we need courage.

Courage

Courage is always an issue of the heart. And when you are at the heart of an issue, you are at what matters most to you. After three hours of storytelling, it was clear I was at a decision point regarding my career and the direction I was heading. It felt like God had been preparing me my whole life for such a season and time as this. As Dave sat and listened to me that day, my soul was nurtured and cared for. We walked through difficult points in my life where I had stumbled, but we also celebrated real successes in my life, which stimulated a heart of gratitude. Somehow in the telling of the story it was becoming clear to both Dave and me that it was the weaving together of all of these stories that was creating quite the picture of where I was to spend my time and helping me to focus my decisions for what was ahead. It was becoming evident that I had a decision before me, and what was required was the courage to step into it.

On the edge of a decision, take only one step at a time. Rarely is the path ever completely laid out, and often the most courageous step is the first one. The easiest way to take that step is if you have someone walking along with you. As a conversationalist, if you've engaged in conversation to this point, you've likely walked with this person beyond the first conversation. You have access to their life and permission to speak into it, which is permission at a heart level.

That first step is often not so much about providing a solution but about helping somebody take that first step. In my case, it was taking a step from a seventeen-year-long career during a down market and a difficult time, knowing I was stewarding something far greater than just operating a business. I had been given a gift as a communicator, as well as a coach, but I didn't really know how to exercise that gift and skill set. Within a month of that conversation in Norway, I'd been given an opportunity to speak and another opportunity to step into a role as an executive coach. I remember the timidity as I stepped into this new direction, wondering, "Can I do this?"

I carried a confidence that was expressed in my abilities and competencies, but I knew all too well the timidity I felt within. This is such a strong charge to discern what is going on at a heart level. Is there a level of timidity, worry, or fear that might be holding that person back? My conversation with Dave over three hours in a farmhouse on the other side of the world actually started eighteen months before when I was first introduced to him. That conversation of prolonged storytelling, of knowing and being known, was actually the tipping point where it became so obvious to me that instead of an affirming exercise of telling my story, it suddenly became one of stewardship. Dave walked with me on that first step.

Why is it that people who aspire for such great things are often the ones who experience the most doubt and fear? It's amazing how we can have the capacity for both. Not everyone struggles with such extremes, yet if you walk closely with somebody during a time of transition, courage is required. And when courage is required, it leaves room for doubt. That is often when we most need those we hold in regard as a confidant, a conversationalist who is ready to impart courage by simply stating and modeling their belief in us. We don't have to look too far for people who have aspired and done great things to see that behind those people are a few others who have stood with them, saying, "I am with you and here for you." Such a commitment inspires us to do things beyond what we thought possible.

When you're at this level, you're in a sacred space that is reserved for only a precious few. Most people guard their hearts from this level of intimacy and trust in relationship, as they should. When you're at this decision point, and you've got a confidant who is there with you and who believes in you, that same person raises the banner, releases the charge, and says, "Go for it! You can do it!"

There's room for inspiration as well as aspiration of who you are, what you are to become, and what you can accomplish. One of the greatest privileges in relationship is when you experience somebody at their deepest point of fear and doubt, then to see them overcome those moments and step forward to see the victory that is the result of their lives as they have an impact on other people. What a joy it is to see in quiet, confidential moments that you were able to be the catalyst for change.

> What a joy it is to see in quiet, confidential moments that you were able to be the catalyst for change.

Knowing and Being Known

Knowing and being known is the high calling of relationships, and the gate to access the heart is discernment. If you're engaged in a relationship where at one time the other person's life seemed blessed with cool, calm waters, but now the flow is at flood stage, be patient. Wait till that season has passed to ask the questions. Until then, care for them in the midst of the flow and pace of their life. Consider the questions you will ask them, that they will have time to process and engage with you, creating a conversational catch.

And finally, as you consider your ability to discern, what helps you create a lens so you can see what is going on below the surface? What can you do to gain a better perspective so you can see, sharpen, and clarify your own thinking? This question is critical as we consider the source of all discernment, which comes from the Spirit of God. He is the one who ultimately provides the care, the counsel, and the courage everyone needs.

Before you engage conversationally with others, take the time to pray, look at the Scriptures, and seek counsel for yourself regarding the questions you should be asking. Whatever your context, circumstance, or level of relationship you find yourself in, whether it is just starting out or a lifetime full of history, being intentional to discern what's going on and engaging in those life-changing questions creates the possibility of a life-changing response. Knowing and being known is what everyone longs for but only a few receive.

INSIGHTS AND ACTIONS

1. Who in your life knows your life story?
2. Who has discerned and helped you in the following ways:
   a. Care (healing a hurt)
   b. Counsel (acquiring wisdom, insight, and understanding)
   c. Courage (overcoming and moving forward)
3. For these three areas of discernment, identify your ability as the following:
   a. Strength
   b. Stretch
   c. Struggle
4. For conversational discernment, identify how you want to grow each of these areas:
   a. The right glasses to see what's going on below the surface
   b. The flies (questions) to initiate the right conversation
   c. The flow to engage in your relationships
5. Regarding counsel, how can you better discern the readiness, teachability, and clarity of the person you're meeting?
6. How often do you take time to pray for your conversations? What conversation do you have coming up this week that you will pray for? Take a moment to pray right now.

Chapter 5

ESSENTIALS TO INCREASE YOUR CONVERSATIONAL CAPACITY

My heart is moved with gratitude as I consider my good friend Richard. I have known him for over fifteen years. Our friendship began as a working relationship, but it now includes building a business together, experiencing financial setbacks, and a move across the country. Now we talk about our fears, our dreams, and our passions. Though distance has separated us for almost twelve years, that relationship stays intact because of a history of a defining season in both of our lives.

Just recently, we talked about the differences between transparency and vulnerability. This man knows what it is to be transparent in front of thousands, yet his vulnerability is limited to only a select few. He told me, "I've only shared this with my wife, and no other, and now I share this with you . . . " Such a statement is an affirmation and a trust that comes through time and history—a connection that's made even in a brief exchange over a significant decision he's facing.

He has given me permission to speak into his life, but more importantly is the opportunity to ask questions that help provide some direction and to unlock the heart of the issue he is struggling with. The issue he is facing is something that is heart-deep and needs to be drawn out, which can only be done through a series of questions that require wisdom, insight, and understanding. To be invited into such a dialogue is a place of honor and a sacred trust. Action steps result from such a conversation, influencing the next three to five years of his life because of the commitment he's making. Only a trusted relationship could guide him through such decisions. How do we acquire relationships like this one?

No matter our relational capacity to have conversations with many or with few, we need a guide as a way of thinking through how to develop our capacity for deeper and more meaningful conversations. We are laying a foundation as preparation, either in a single conversation or one that is developed over a decade. The old axiom of being a mile wide and an inch deep illustrates the challenge for all of us, that we have capacity to go deeper in our relationships. And we get there by developing conversational capacities in five areas: trust, authenticity, vulnerability, availability, and commitment.

These five areas provide us a grid for thinking about how we develop a strong capacity, a discernment for where we may be relationally challenged, and a guide for how we can improve in every engagement. Capacity also has to do with knowing our limitations, for the problem of being a mile wide and an inch deep has to do with boundaries. Where are the limitations we need to put in place so that we are not spread so thin that we lose all our energy, our mental and emotional capacity to go deeper?

In the fall of 2007, I was in the best physical shape of my life. I had just completed the Colorado Springs Triple Crown Series, which included a 10K run at Bear Creek, a ten-mile run at the Garden of the Gods, and the capstone of the series was the half marathon known as the Pikes Peak Ascent. The run up Pikes Peak begins at a six thousand–foot elevation and ends at over fourteen thousand feet, covering thirteen miles of treacherous terrain. At the top with my family celebrating, I felt a sense of personal accomplishment; yet if you would have told me two months from that pinnacle I would be flat on my back in the hospital with pneumonia, I would have never believed you.

With the combination of running a business, building a home, beginning the process of homeschooling our kids, and a host of other commitments, my stress level was at an all-time high. In some ways, it revealed a physical vulnerability that took me from the best shape of my life to the worst. The physical reality of pneumonia affects your capacity to take in oxygen, so that every time you take a breath your lungs are not receiving the amount of necessary oxygen to sustain your body. Even though I was in the hospital for only three days, it impacted my ability to function at full capacity for months to come.

The idea of capacity has more than physical implications, however; it affects us emotionally, mentally, spiritually, financially, and, of course, relationally. If you are going through a season right now of extreme difficulty, you may be in a time of brokenness that absolutely affects your capacity to engage relationally. And that's okay. When the time is right, you can begin to take baby steps toward engaging in meaningful and life-giving relationships.

In addition, it helps you understand how to draw out people who are in similar situations. If you've experienced an extreme season, either in your life or in your work, you may be in a time of burnout where there's just nothing left in the tank to give. We've all experienced times like that when the demands of life seem to be more than we can manage. Capacity is a real issue, and we have to evaluate our capacity to give.

You may also be at a point where you are ready to engage in fresh, dynamic relationships, moving beyond the trivial of everyday conversations—you want to move to more of a heart level. You're ready for a relational breakthrough. Whether you find yourself in a place of brokenness or burnout, longing for a breakthrough, my hope is that you are given the framework to think about how to develop your capacity toward life-changing relationships.

The depth of your conversational capacity is situational. There are many times we have those rare and wonderful experiences where we sit at a table with someone and, before we know it, an hour has gone by—it seemed like only a few minutes. We have an ability to connect and find common points of interest that are so life-giving that, even though we may have only met them for the first time, we enjoy their company and look forward to our next time together. On the other extreme, we also know the feeling of sitting down with somebody and in only a few minutes it feels painful to be with that person. No matter how well we navigate the questions, finding points of connection or interest, we feel like we are suffocating conversationally.

During the season when I had pneumonia, it wasn't until I actually got to the hospital and was given the right medication that began increasing my white blood cell count that I felt like I had been given a supercharged dose of adrenaline. Every time I took a breath I was getting oxygen in places where I needed; whereas, for the month prior every time I took a breath I was gasping for air. In no way was I ready to go out and conquer another Pikes Peak Ascent. In fact, it would be months before I could even get on the treadmill or do any sustained physical activity. But by the springtime, I was back running at a pace of 10–15 miles per week.

Capacity is something you don't really know until you engage with other people. No matter where you are at today, whether you are engaged in life-giving relationships or working with people who are more difficult, you have an ability to expand your capacity for life-changing relationships. In addition, as that person goes through a difficult circumstance, you are able to take the time for a few well-meaning conversations, which is part of walking alongside them till they turn the corner circumstantially and their world changes. And it's through those moments that you have the potential for a lifelong friendship simply because you walked with them through such a time of difficulty.

Your perseverance and walking alongside somebody to the

point where they are spurred on toward love and good deeds—where their life is no longer just about their self-interests, but now they have a vision to go and have an impact in other's people lives—creates joy in the conversationalist. You get to experience the joy of seeing that person's life turn around. This is the foundation for friendship. The greater the conversational capacity you have, the greater you increase your potential for friendship in the future.

Trust

Trust comes in three different ways: it is acquired, it is given, or it is earned. In the case of my friendship, all three of these of these are present.

Trust Is Acquired

For those who acquire such trust, it's done through time, history, and experience. That experience can come through shared common experiences, such as growing up in the same grade school or the same church or going to college together. You could have been in the same youth group, going to youth camps in the summertime, or you could have gone to same fall retreats. Such moments can be defining experiences. One of the greatest of these is having and raising your children together during the same time, being a part of a small group, or experiencing regular date nights where friends share the responsibility of watching each other's kids so they can have date nights.

It could be starting a business together that either succeeded or failed. Moving into a new city and finding one of your first friendships in a neighborhood, in a church, or on a sports team develops this type of trust as well. I found that in the most vulnerable seasons of life circumstantially, those relationships who walked alongside us during those times have a trust in our lives because of those experiences, which we can now speak to and draw upon in conversation. This is a reminder of where we've been and who we were, which gives indication to where we're going.

Trust Is Given

Trust given is most easily understood by us. When we have someone who is referred to us as a doctor, and who is able to help in a time of need, we meet with that specialist who can understand our pain and situation and can speak into that, potentially even diagnosing and offering some prescriptive solutions. We may also find such a relationship in a pastor or a counselor, who has experience in such matters. Because of their reputation, which comes because of their character and faithfulness, we are able to trust them to speak into our lives.

As a facilitator of teams, I've had the opportunity to come into an organization and be able to have permission to ask questions and speak into a leader and team regarding the issues at hand. Such a place of trust can only be given to a person. Since this type of trust is given, we must not move conversationally beyond that which we have been given permission to speak into.

For those whose trust has been given, we may offer some insight from experience, discernment, or training; for those who have given such trust, they may not be ready to receive the level of insight you have. Such is the difference in protecting this trust, a difference of approach on giving prescriptive solutions versus asking questions to draw out the heart. The listening actually earns greater trust just by taking the time to honor the person who's sharing.

Trust Is Earned

Most people I meet have experienced some level of broken trust, putting some people in the category of skeptics or cynics. Regardless of their attitude, however, they are rightfully protective of giving away trust too quickly. Most of us are in situations—whether it's a small group within a church context or a team within an organization—where we don't have time to build years of history. We have a project, a task, or a study that we're doing that will be accomplished in a matter of weeks. We have to have some sort of working relationship and therefore some level of working trust.

Any time there is a challenge on the table, there's an opportunity for trust to be earned. People can step into that challenge, and how they perform within the midst of that challenge lends itself to a credibility that did not exist before. Such a challenge may create relational friction, and thus a conflict may arise. How people handle the conflict is important: whether they are defensive and argumentative, or whether they seek some higher ground for mutual agreement and resolution. Witnesses to such an event are paying close attention to the individuals involved. How they handle themselves lends to whether they will earn the trust of those who are watching.

> Any time there is a challenge on the table, there's an opportunity for trust to be earned.

This applies to leaders who are stepping into organizations for the first time. Members of such an organization are watching to see how the leader is going to respond to challenges as well as the conflicts that arise. If a leader responds with excellence and an attitude that's life-giving and serving, rather than self-seeking, then it lends itself to building trust with those who see it. There are reservoirs of trust, which are the equity of relationships. Before we really engage and press into relationships, we must know the equity of such a relationship.

If trust has not been acquired, if we go to draw upon such an equity, we may find that there's not much within that well to draw from. Questions such as, "How are you doing?" and the trite response of "Just fine" over a period of months may be misunderstood to imply that the person is shallow and doesn't have much to offer. However, the person responding to a courteous question isn't ready to engage at a level beyond saying they are fine.

Here's where we get into trouble in relationships, because we presume this person either lacks a depth or has an inability to engage at such a depth that the person asking desires to go to. But nothing could be further from the truth. The person who shows a consistent model of taking a few extra minutes over a cup of coffee to see what's happening and clearly listening and engaging will build greater trust. That person shows a consistency of modeling, a care and a concern, and an ability to engage wherever he or she is at in the moment. When that caring person asks the same person how they're doing, it's more than, "I'm fine." The respondent actually engage at another level because they know the sincerity of those who are asking.

We've all been in similar situations, whether we're the one asking or the ones being asked. The level of your response often has much to do with the level of trust you have in the person asking the question. Such an example could be contrasted with an old friend, whom you haven't talked to in five or ten years, and suddenly you're reacquainted. Because there was a trust level there before, the equity of relationship has not been damaged, and that allows you to go to a level that is life-giving and refreshing, where both of you are surprised how quickly you can go to a depth you haven't experienced in years.

Every one of us has a need and desire to be cared for, even though how that's expressed can be done in many different ways. The truth is that all of us are built for loving relationships. Such loving relationships go to the very heart of who we are, and it's within that place we find the capacity to trust. Such trust is built on a foundation of knowing and being known.

Regardless of whether you're an introvert or an extrovert, you are built for relationships. Some people may be built to only go deep with a few, while others may have the capacity to go deep with many more. Your capacity for such relationships has much to do with your capacity to trust. I have found many people over the years who have been violated in one form or another, and they make a vow to never trust again. An example of this is people who are surrounded by other people and yet feel totally alone. Where do such feelings come from?

There are many who have learned to mask their insecurities through their jobs and other material things, such as clothing, cars, and houses. Such a lifestyle can superficially cover the heart that is anxious and insecure. The challenge for the conversationalist, however, is that questions filled with love and sincerity and built on trust will access the heart and potentially reveal an insecurity. Yet this where love is given and administered to those in need. My friend who is transparent among thousands, yet vulnerable to only a few doesn't need to be vulnerable with thousands, nor does he have the ability to be, but his vulnerability with a few allows him the security to be transparent.

The challenge of the conversationalist is not about having depth of relationships with the many; rather, it is about having that type of relationship with the few, developing deepening levels of trust, transparency, and vulnerability with the people you already have in your life. These questions will help provide a framework for you to build relationships through conversations that will ultimately bring about life change through discovery and development, awakening what matters most in your life.

Authenticity

Model authenticity. For me, there are certain expressions or clichés that trigger responses of cynicism and borderline sarcasm. I am sharing this as a bit of a confession. Such responses early in conversation either help me engage or cause me to question the sincerity of the individual I'm talking to. One such expression is, "I'm living the dream!" Sometimes people say that comment and I think, "Man, I know your life, and you're a mess. You're not living the dream!" I'm not saying their life is a nightmare, but it's certainly not "the dream." The comments made in some cliché way parrot an idea somebody else has expressed, but it really poses as a cover-up for their own insecurity or not really knowing what they think or feel. Either way, I have some twinge of my own rejection and think, "Man, come on. Be real!" When I boil it down; what repels me is when people aren't real.

Modeling authenticity in appropriate ways sets the conversational tone, whether it's one-on-one, in a family, in a small group, or even within an organizational context. It sets the culture you are trying to create. Rather than deflecting with cliché statements, we have the opportunity to communicate early in the conversation with a level of sincerity and in ways that leave the door open for the possibility of that person expressing something of equal sincerity to our comment.

I'm not suggesting that every comment authentically needs to be some downer; in fact, I want to be careful on this point, because there are circles of people I have encountered who remind me a little bit of Eeyore. By no means am I suggesting we should all be a bunch of Tiggers; but if we are in a room full of Eeyores, it can get really depressing pretty fast. Whichever character you best resonate with, responding at a point of sincerity in a personal way that is authentic for you is what people respond to. One of the greatest ways to do this is through story.

The craftsmanship of the conversationalist is the ability to tell stories in appropriate ways within the time frame you have available that connects with your listener. You're not just telling the story for the sake of the story, but so that further dialogue may be provoked with the people you are with. Let me illustrate this in regard to something that most of us have experienced. Regardless of the content or agenda that's being shared, we have a funny way of leaning in a little bit more when a personal story is being shared. We're more engaged and attentive to the details because it's something that we can relate to, something more than just information we are trying to acquire.

Your ability to be able to tell stories in personable and sincere ways, without completely hijacking the conversation, leaves a door wide open for others to respond and relate in similar ways. A story reciprocated gives you a window into that person's life, their thoughts and attitudes, and helps you respond in a way that gives you some cues of where you need to go or want to go conversationally. Authenticity is a capacity builder because it's something that, as it becomes a part of your rhythm and normal interactions with people, builds your reputation as an authentic person and someone who brings themselves fully into every engagement. Just as when you are listening to someone publically present, their sincerity sets you at ease into the flow of whatever is being presented. The same thing happens conversationally—when you present a story, it helps set people at ease even though their story may represent some level of difficulty.

Authenticity breaks down pretense. We often don't really know where to engage. We don't know what comments are appropriate, or sometimes even the questions to ask, but authenticity gives us a foundation through story, and our response allows us to press in through well-meaning questions and responses. As you are looking at increasing your relational capacity, one of the greatest ways you can start is by increasing levels of authenticity, looking for ways to articulate your story and other points that are personable with a level of sincerity.

Authenticity breaks down pretense.

As we move through the ideas of the conversationalist, it could be implied that we are trying to relate to every point of interest, opinion, or idea of those we are conversing with. And yet if we do so like a chameleon, trying to morph what we think, feel, or believe with every person we are with, then we will miss something. There is something to be said for being authentically you in every conversation you have.

In the context of building relational capacity, if your goal is to be authentic just to get your point across every time, that's one of the fastest ways to relationally disengage. Authenticity has to do with the points that make you *you*. Take food, for example. If you have some personal favorites and you let people know, that may not necessarily be what they want to have in the moment, but when it comes time for your birthday, and everyone knows that's what you love, it's a way for them to celebrate you. And you can do the same for others.

The more authentic we are, and the more we bring that authenticity into our relationships, the more it gives potential for greater common ground and a depth to form because they are the things we value. This is what makes us unique. As you bring who you are fully into a conversation, it models the same for those who are with you. As you think about authenticity, it's less about what's shared or not shared and more about you being fully authentic in the relationships that you have.

Where do you find yourself being insincere, impersonal, or just outright presenting a persona of how you want people to see you? If you're struggling in your relationships, in your connecting at a deeper level, it may be time to break some of these patterns. As we continue to grow in our ability of authenticity, it increases our ability to engage with people and moves us to the next capacity builder: vulnerability.

Vulnerability

It's often our greatest point of weakness that reveals our greatest potential for strength. Early in my coaching career, I was sitting with a leader who was building up to something that I could tell was difficult for him. It wasn't any point of great secrecy or compromise; it was simply something he hadn't shared with anyone before. By every standard he was successful, well respected, and financially well off, yet his comment represented an insecurity he had felt most of his life. After I had listened, I asked if he had ever shared that with anyone before, which he had not. And after some further discussion, I asked if he would be open to sharing with a few other leaders who could affirm him and encourage him in that area of his life. "No way," he said sharply, with a look like I was crazy.

The point of vulnerability and the courage he had to share with me was a huge breakthrough, yet his insecurity had no real foundation, other than it was something that he believed about himself. It was a lie, and he needed to have some truth spoken over him. The point of vulnerability and the weakness it represents stays a weakness as long as it has a hold on your life. Once that vulnerability is exposed, however, more often than not it becomes a strength because you've chosen to resource it with love and truth, and a few people who will help you walk through it.

Ultimately, the difference between authenticity and the line of vulnerability is when you move along the story, from how you felt to the point where you can acknowledge your own need. It's one thing to be sincere, and sincerity is endearing to relationships, yet vulnerability is done more often in closer circles of the most trusted relationships. This is where you lay down your pride and acknowledge your own need, even to the point of asking for help. Doing this moves you to a place of humility.

Trust is certainly essential for all of the reasons already expressed, and authenticity creates the further potential for relationship. Yet I can't think of another thing that has as great a potential for life-changing implications than the humility of being vulnerable, expressing your need, and asking for help. I've heard it said that if we cannot express our need, then it makes it impossible for people to truly love us.

As we talk about building capacity for relationships, we are at a level of intimacy that is rarely experienced by most people today. Yet when we can express our need as conversationalists, we honor the people in our life by not placing a false hope that they are going to fulfill our need. Rather, their seeing us express the point of vulnerability allows them to do the same. And, more importantly, vulnerability gets to the heart of relationship.

The expression of your vulnerability has to be done in context with who you are with, because the weight of your issue may far exceed the ability of those listeners to respond in appropriate ways. One of the greatest places this can be done is within a home environment, like a parent and child. You don't necessarily have to go into the full details of why something carries such a weight, but this gives you the opportunity to express the emotions around those ideas. And for every moment you can acknowledge a sadness, the next day it may give you the opportunity to express joy.

Creating a balance of expressing what is felt allows your children to help process what they are feeling as well. As a parent, you can respond in appropriate levels, starting first with a hug.

One of the most beautiful moments in a family is having your children respond by making one of those crayon cards with a picture of them holding your hand as a couple of stick figures on a page, with "I love you, Daddy!" scribbled on the page. Expressing your need in appropriate levels of detail in the context of who you are with allows people to reciprocate by resourcing that need. Conversely, not expressing anything to anyone isolates you from receiving the much-needed care that allows you to be healthy, thus leaving your weakness still your weakness.

If is an area in which you want to grow your capacity, then I would encourage you to look at the people in your life who represent a healthy balance of vulnerability as they express their need and model a humility in their life. Spending time with those people and learning from their modeling impacts you to the point where you can do the same as a conversationalist. As you consider these three areas of capacity builders—trust, authenticity, and vulnerability—any engagement in one or all three of these areas has the potential to change the landscape of your relationships and how you engage in conversations. This moves us to the fourth capacity builder: availability.

Availability

As a conversationalist, you can model a wonderful capacity to be trustworthy, authentic, and even vulnerable, and yet if you are limited in your availability, then your capacity for life-changing relationships will be limited as well. Are you spending time doing the most important things, or are the most important things getting your second best? Nobody intends to be the kind of person who gives their priorities second best, yet the demands and realities of life have a tendency to move our daily grind to where we respond to the urgent. And, before we know it, we wake up, whether it's a few weeks, months, or even years later, and our best is getting second-hand efforts.

If we take the time to look at the names of the people we most care about in our lives, and who are getting the dregs of our efforts, it will break our heart. When we look at the most important people who are in our life, in our family, friendships, and even in our work setting, those people experience us with a Do Not Disturb sign on the door of our heart. Availability has to do with a lot more than just our time and our schedule. Much subtler, but just as real, is the issue of our emotional and mental availability.

We live in a culture that often finds its significance and identity from busyness. Whether our efforts are actually productive is beside the point. It's often in the perception of busyness that we find our significance. And ultimately, our question is, are we busy with the right things? We need to evaluate what the priorities in our life are, who we need to be more present with, and who needs access to our time, our thoughts, and our heartfelt consideration. Also, what is causing our fatigue and our exhaustion?

The temptation is always once we meet this quarterly goal, or we get beyond this event, or once we get to our family vacation, or at some time in the future, then we will suddenly produce an abundance of time to give to what matters most. But you and I both know the limitations and lies in such thinking.

If we are going to create space in our time, our thinking, and even in our cares, then we are likely going to have to say no to some very good things. Limiting our commitments to some secondary priorities in order to recalibrate our lives to what matters most (or, rather, *who* matters most) is what is needful here. As you go through this process of proactively creating some space in your life, this will allow you to be more present and engaged with those around you, and doing so will allow you to order your life in a way that you have some margin so that you can clearly communicate your availability and your commitment to that person. This allows you to evaluate what time you have available to commit to that person, whether that's a weekly date night with your spouse, a regular meeting with your executive team, or a bit of planning with one of your friends.

Considering your availability allows you to clearly communicate what you can or cannot commit to. We are finite creatures, and there is a big world out there with a whole lot of need. As a friend of mine articulates, the need does not determine the call. Just because you are surrounded by people who want to engage you doesn't mean you need to or should. You need to take time to regularly consider your commitments of how much time and investment you are pouring into people and where you may be limited. The point of determining your capacity is more about you evaluating relationships and your availability than just your calendar.

Commitment

During that season of pneumonia, I experienced perpetual exhaustion. There were times I could barely walk up the stairs, even though I had just climbed a mountain. As conversationalists, we all have an unbelievable ability to engage relationally, yet we must know our time and season when we need to catch our breath because we are exhausted. Our momentary condition may put us on the sidelines for a time, but that should not be indicative of completely disengaging from the most important people in our lives. As we take time to create availability, it prepares our heart and our mind, as well as the practicality of our calendar, in the clarity of our commitments.

Clarifying commitments and creating trust go hand in hand. When we depend on people who make commitments that we are dependent on, these either break down or build up our capacity for relationships. Just as you evaluate your availability, you have to create margin for what and who is a priority in your life. Often, the relationships that experience the greatest level of disappointment are the ones that had unrealistic expectations. But it is important to recognize that those expectations came from somewhere.

As we grow in our maturity as conversationalists, we need to take the time to evaluate what we are communicating with people and then overcommunicate those ideas to make sure we are not leaving ourselves exposed to unrealistic expectations. When we don't take the time to clarify our commitments, it lends itself to an insecurity in the relationship, which can then result in people overperforming, seeking to please, or even withdrawing.

The commitment we are referring to has to do with the security that comes from a relationship not built on performance. We all have to do something to engage in the relationship, and to withdraw from conversation only shuts down the equity of the relationship. When you take time to commit to a relationship, it adds a security that minimizes the volatility or ambiguity of trying to figure out what people are thinking or feeling. Even if your commitment is minimal, you still value and honor that person by clarifying how you will walk alongside him or her. Again, this ranges from formal to informal, personal and professional. Clarifying your commitments adds a security to the relationship that lends itself to deeper conversations that may not happen otherwise.

INSIGHTS AND ACTIONS

1. When in your life have you felt a mile wide and an inch deep, relationally speaking? What factors were influencing your isolation?

2. Building a conversational capacity is a lifetime pursuit. Start today by being more intentional and developing your ability to connect deeper with every interaction. Evaluate and commit to one of the five capacity builders you will exhibit this week:

   • Trust (modeling maturity—being relaxed, at peace, and competent)

- Authenticity (telling story—being sincere, personal, and relatable)
- Vulnerability (expressing need—being humble, approachable, and helpful)
- Availability (inviting access—having priorities, being present, and presenting margin)
- Commitment (clarifying expectations—participating, dependable, accountable)

3. How can you trust God for where your conversations need to go?

4. Work with your conversationalist partner to evaluate specific interactions for affirmation and improvement for your next time together. Then select the next capacity builder and integrate it into further discussions.

Chapter 6

LEADING PEOPLE TO THEIR OWN DISCOVERY

Over the last four years as an executive coach, I have learned the discipline of leading people to their own discovery. The temptation in any conversation is to hear what's going on and then try to fix it, so that it either relieves the other person's pain or releases their potential to discover the possibilities that are before them. The conversationalist helps unlock life-changing relationships through meaningful, engaging conversations.

We all desire to have meaningful conversations that have the potential for life-changing implications. Yet how do we get into such conversations and move beyond the trivial, mundane, or cliché answers, to really keep people from what we are thinking or feeling? In this chapter we are going to discuss a discovery process using seven questions that act as a lead-in to warm up the conversation, taking you from the surface level to what matters most in a person's life. These seven questions are a guide that will help you in the discovery process, as well as help those you are conversing with.

The principle of discovery is that people take action more on what they realize than what they are told to do. As a conversationalist, your key role is leading others to their own discovery, which will ultimately impact their own perspective, attitude, and actions. For those who are still asking how to get the conversation started toward life-changing conversations, these seven questions provide a framework that will lead you further into dialogue that gets to the heart.

Conversation Continuum
7 Discovery Questions

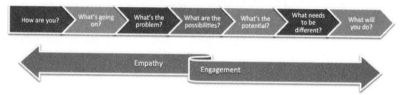

It's a continuum of conversations that will ground you in the discussion. Every question moves you from empathy to engagement. You're discerning the care in casual conversation to spurring on as a catalyst for real change. As we enter uncommon conversations, we are at the heart level, talking at levels that often may never have been explored or expressed. These seven questions will give you a guide for how to navigate the conversation to the next level within a few minutes or over a few months. As each question is answered with sincerity and significance, that will give you the cue to ask the next question. If the answers need further discovery, then patiently take the time and explore the depth on just one of the seven. The continuum will guide and set the pace and intensity for moving the conversation forward. Let's begin the discovery.

Question #1: How Are You?

When this question is asked of us, 95 percent of us say, "I'm fine." More often than not, that answer rolls right off the tongue. That's what we are patterned to say when asked, because it's a general greeting like, "Nice day to you" or "Good morning." "How are you?" is a general acknowledgement that you are there and I am here. Although it's framed as a question, it's really more of a statement than anything else. We often respond quickly when asked this question because we don't share how we really are (and besides, we are not really sure if the person asking even cares to know anyhow). Even if they did care to know how we were really doing, the greeting in the elevator or through a quick passing doesn't lend itself to a long conversation.

I am always tickled with this idea of someone saying they are fine, because it reminds me of a scene in the movie *Italian Job*, when Mark Wahlberg and Donald Sutherland are talking in Venice before their heist. Sutherland says, "You know what *fine* means? Freaked out, insecure, neurotic, and emotional." If we actually expressed how we are doing in a casual greeting, then those words may come out with a lot more detail and a whole lot more than the person asking was ready to engage with. There is a tragic reality that we're probably not doing as well as we let on.

The conversationalist, however, pays attention to how the other person is really doing. Even in a casual exchange, he or she can pick up from the gestures, the tone of voice, or even the facial expressions that something may seem amiss. We may respond with something like, "I don't know what it is, but something seems a bit different about you today" or "I saw on Facebook that you posted about your family (or an event you did)," giving a little cue that we are paying attention to the details of their lives, which gives an indication that we would really like to know how they are doing. Somewhere within this first question is the launchpad for the conversationalist to look at later questions, thus opening up possibilities.

> The conversationalist pays attention to how the other person is really doing.

The decision of whether we want to move forward with how we are really doing actually shows the level of care for that person. Do we want to take the time to listen to what's going on in their life? In some ways, this question represents the riskiest of the seven questions because we don't know what we are going to get. Is there a struggle going on at home, did that person get passed over for a promotion, or did they just get a diagnosis from their doctor and they're not sure how to handle it?

Some may view this question as an inconvenience, but that is not what it is—I don't just want to offer a greeting in order to acknowledge that person, but I want to actually engage with what is happening under the surface. How many people do you have in your life that you can honestly say care about you and what's going on in your life, beyond the question of how you're doing? This is the threshold for the conversationalist moving to the next level in a relationship. It is also the beginning of the conversation continuum, which is empathy.

With every question and conversation point, we move further along the continuum, from empathy to engagement. And this is certainly more than a theoretical or philosophical point. Rather, this is the working out of the conversationalist. Consider your day today. How many people will you meet with? How many people will you ask the question, "How are you?" and how many will reply, "I am fine"? You have the opportunity to actually press forward into the conversationalist continuum and move on to the next question.

Question #2: What's Going On?

As we move beyond the first question of greeting and connection, we come into the second question that deals with the details of what's happening in a person's life. It's the natural progression in normal conversation that cues us to go deeper with them and lets us know they're ready to share what's going on. It's amazing how people feel cared for when you're able to listen and then repeat the details of what's happening in that person's life.

There was a funny video that came out a few years ago on YouTube about shallow small groups. It says that we're okay saying, "Hey, bud," or walking up to a guy and saying, "Hey, bro, what's up?" The irony of the shallow small group is that it's okay if we don't know each other's name. Compare this with *Cheers*, the popular sitcom of the '80s, "where everybody knows your name." When you meet somebody, you actually use their name and say, "Hey, Steve, what's going on?" When you use the details of what's been shared with you up to that point in the conversation, you personalize what's been happening, and you show that person that they are valued, they've been heard, and you care about the specifics of what's happening in their life. As a conversationalist, you can frame further questions around the details of what they have shared with you.

Just recently I sat with a dear friend who has been a mentor for me. He and his wife, to whom he has been married for fifty-three years, came in from Southern California and we had dinner together. The purpose of their trip was to visit family; more specifically, they were going up to northern Colorado to visit her brother, who is struggling with the effects of Alzheimer's. My part to play in the conversation was certainly not to fix anything but to listen to the details of what was going on and to listen to some of the stories of her brother's life, which honored them both as she was truly grieving for her brother. At that moment, my part to play in the conversation was to give empathy, and one of the greatest ways I could do that was by intently listening to what was going on in her life.

As you look around at the circle of your relationships, you don't have to go too far to see people hurting, whether it is because of some financial setbacks, a parent struggling with their children, or a medical issue. There are certainly times to engage the conversation further into discovery, but then one of the most honoring things we can do is to have the discernment to know when that person needs to simply be cared for.

One of the greatest ways we can engage that relationship and those defining moments is to listen to the details of the stories of those people's lives and then ask questions around those details in ways that show a genuine care and concern for them. Thus we build a stronger foundation for relationships for the present as well as for the future. Who knows, maybe we are the person on the other end who has experienced a setback or some unwelcome news, and we need some comfort by that person listening to the details of our life.

> Listen to the details of the stories of people's lives and then ask questions in ways that show a genuine care and concern for them.

As we move forward in the conversation continuum from empathy to engagement, it's important to remember once again people don't care how much you know until they know how much you care. As we transition to question three, much discernment is needed. There should be a warning label on knowing when to move to the next question: if that person is in a place where they need to sit a little while longer in the disappointment of the moment, then let the conversation rest. But if you sense that they are ready to move forward, then do so with question number three.

Question #3: What's the Problem?

We're moving conversationally from connection to defining what is going on to clarifying the challenge that a person is presently facing. The old adage says, "A problem defined is half solved." Referring to the circles of significant conversations, we are still in the contextual realm of seeking to understand what's truly going on in another's life.

I have no professional training as a mediator, but oftentimes I come in and facilitate as an objective third-party voice at the table. When I've served in this role, there is typically a certain amount of volatility expressed through a high amount of emotions by either of the parties. Before all the parties have to come to the table, a discovery has to be made. Through an interview process that focuses on the expectations of the relationship, the mutual commitment, what has been broken, what's at stake, what their agenda is, and if they are open to restoration of the relationship, a discovery is made. This is certainly a more formal approach, but when you're working with high-stakes challenges, a more formal approach to discovery is required so you can have a more complete understanding of all the details and variables.

As a coach, I will often ask a leader, "Can you monetize this issue?" It's amazing how you can walk through several issues in a short period of time to define the problems or challenges. And then putting a financial impact on it helps determine the weight and priority of each of these issues. It allows an order of significance when you actually see how much this problem costs you in terms of your time or money. If you are dealing with a problem that doesn't necessarily have a direct financial tie to it, consider the value of your time. How much time is this issue taking up in your life? How much mental and emotional energy, or relational equity, is this costing you?

There's a certain discipline of discovery that's required here. The more you get clarity on what the issues or challenges are at hand, the more often you have a response to immediately jump onto a solution. But taking time to explore other perspectives is well worth the wait. Remember that we are seeking to understand what the problem is, so in the most practical application to this question we can explore conversationally whether we're asking the right questions.

As we explore a variety of questions to seek clarity and understanding, a final question to help ground the issue is this: On a scale of 1–10, what is the emotional weight of this issue? When you can go through and create a list of the issues (whether it's one issue or multiple issues) then evaluate the weight of that issue from an emotional standpoint, this helps give you a grounding from which to operate. More often than not we lose objectivity the more emotional the issue becomes, and thus our clarity suffers as a result.

As we move down the conversation continuum from empathy to engagement, we are actually moving toward a level of objectivity to guide people in their discovery. Such a discovery process of clarifying the issue and defining the problem often results in an awareness that wasn't there before. With this perspective refreshed, we have a better understanding and put words to things that have caused us anxiety, thus relieving a burden and lightening our step to get us ready to move forward.

Question #4: What Are the Possibilities?

Here's the midpoint of our continuum from empathy to engagement. You might even call it a tipping point, which is ultimately where our perspective shifts. It's the threshold from being preoccupied with the problems of the past to possessing clarity of what's going on in the present and moving us forward to the possibility of what lies ahead.

I am a huge advocate of Cliftons's StrengthsFinder by Gallup. They measure thirty-four talent themes that represent natural energizing activities. Five years ago, I took the questionnaire for the first time, when I was in a different career. Coming out of a difficult work season, I recently retook the StrengthsFinder assessment to see a comparison of my top five talents. I went from a place of burnout to where I am now: living out the full expression of my strengths and talents on a daily basis. The assessment scored four of my five talents in the same way, and, ironically, in the same order. One of those characteristics is ideation, which means I love to brainstorm; it's one of my greatest joys to explore with others the possibilities of their situation, given their current circumstances.

When we move the conversation from present problems to future possibilities, it gets us dreaming once again. One of the greatest places of trust in relationships is built when people share their dreams with us. More often than not, dreams are not really that clear, so when you can guide people through a discovery process of the possibilities of their future, they begin dreaming once again. As conversationalists, we are helping people discover their dreams. Most people have never really had the time or the relationships to brainstorm about their future possibilities, whether it is for them personally or for their family or work life.

My number one StrengthsFinder result is futuristic, which

means not only do I like to ideate but I also like to think about the future possibilities for people. This is deeply personal, because I believe that our present pain shapes our future possibilities. When we can help people conversationally explore this pain, their present weakness will one day become a strength that will be used for the benefit to other people. This opens up places in their minds and hearts that they may have never thought about before. Some naysayers may bemoan this discipline of discovery into future possibilities because it puts too many ideas into someone else's head and puts them beyond any sort of rational thinking—a place where the normally steady person is now on a wild crusade.

That may be true for a few outliers, but for the most part people need time and space to consider what-if scenarios. What if we did this? What is the possibility if we were to explore that? How would you feel if we went on this trip? What would it be like if you put this story into a book? What if you started that blog? What if you started that program at church? What if you bought that business or started another one?

To dream is what makes us human. When dreams and the possibilities for our future have been drowned out by the mundane routine and prolonged periods of discouragement, we lose what it is to truly be us. As a conversationalist, one of the greatest things you can do is unlock the possibilities by giving a person room to dream and consider the future.

Again, as we are moving along the path of progression from defining problems, a certain level of empathy turns the corner to engagement, so that others can explore their road ahead. This is more than just an intellectual exercise. Seeing themselves in a future state creates an epiphany of sorts: it helps define their circles of influence or encourages them to make a change that really aligns with their authentic purpose. I have witnessed people exploring the possibilities of their lives and

> One of the greatest things you can do is unlock the possibilities by giving a person room to dream and consider the future.

then—months and years later—experiencing the reality of what was just a dream. When you can be a witness of such moments, there is no greater joy.

Question #5: What's the Potential?

Depending on the context of your conversation, you may already be far enough along to consider the plans of the road ahead. Somewhere within exploration is the idea of the potential, the pathway, and the plans to get there. I live in Colorado, and nearly every day I see the purple mountain majesty of Pike's Peak. On almost any given day, between sunrises and sunsets, there are different colors that highlight the mountain, and I can tell you from experience that there is a big difference between looking at and discovering the possibilities of climbing that mountain by studying maps, aerial footage, talking to people who have done so, and looking at photos. I could discover all the possible scenarios of climbing Pike's Peak, yet all the discovery takes on another level of significance when I actually set foot on the mountain.

When we move from empathy to engagement, we're embarking on an adventure to go where we've never gone before. And as with anything in life—whether it's going to a new school, attending a new church, moving to a new city, starting a new job, or anything that moves us out of our comfort zone—it always involves the possibilities of a variety of scenarios. Yet when we take that step of faith to begin exploring the potential of that idea becoming a reality, then we're getting a lot closer to true life change. In the case of Pike's Peak, all the pictures you can see on the Internet are absolutely beautiful, but there is no comparison to when you are standing on that peak after you have hiked thirteen miles.

When you move from discovery to exploring as a conversationalist, you are actually taking all the possibilities that you surfaced, then you're narrowing the other person's focus to define next steps in their exploration. Exploring is a lot like vacationing. It doesn't necessarily mean you want to move there, but you still want to see what it's like going to a new place. When you actually do go, it opens up your world. Sometimes when we feel a nudge toward something, it doesn't necessarily mean that it's our pathway for the future, but there may be something within that experience that is a piece of the key to what lies in the path before us.

Stepping into the experience unlocks the potential for a future reality that we didn't even think was possible just by having a key piece of the story open up for us. That could be a new relationship or a new idea, a new perspective or a new strategy. My daughter is getting ready to go to college. We could certainly send her to the local school here, but there is some value in exploring different campuses and seeing what she likes about each one that helps her narrow what she's looking for in her college experience, whether in regard in her major, her interests in athletics, the community and campus life, her friends who may be going to the school, and how far away from home she wants to be.

The same may be true of someone starting a business. One of the best things an entrepreneur can do—once they understand their business concept, strategy, and unique value proposition—is to begin exploring some different organizations and leaders who can speak into the process. It's a whole lot different reading campus journals and business case studies than actually walking on the ground where you're heading. As a conversationalist, after you explore those possibilities, you then guide the conversations to narrow the next steps toward the potential pathway or plan for the person's future. Then we are heading for question number six.

Question #6: What Needs to Be Different?

Personal confession: this is one of the hardest questions for me from an engagement standpoint. I am a high-energy, internal optimist who thinks I can just keep adding and adding to my plate without making any changes. To break it down and make it practical for all of us, for every yes in our life we have got to start saying no to something else.

A friend of mine pastors a church, but he started out as a junior high pastor. His competency was off the charts, and soon he became the pastor for both the high school and the junior high. Then he was given the opportunity to lead the college-age internship program, and from the internship he took on an adjunct position as a seminary professor. He is quite a gifted speaker, so now he spends his time traveling the country as he gets invitations to speak. Did I mention that he is a father of two young kids? Do you see what is happening here? His story is not unique. Highly competent and energetic leaders keep taking on more and more responsibility, and then one day they crash and burn. This doesn't necessarily come from compromise, but from the sheer exhaustion of not being able to keep up the pace over the long term.

As conversationalists, we can guide the conversation by evaluating the opportunity cost. We've just gone through a stimulating process of dreaming about the possibilities and narrowing our focus to the potential path and plan that is before us, and now we need to move the conversation to evaluate what changes need to happen. If we committed to that new opportunity, what's the impact going to be on us, on our family, and on our work? This is more than just an economic consideration; it is a relational impact. Is the possibility of more money but less time with your family worth the cost? As I have observed people who have stepped into new jobs or careers, it's amazing how they underestimated the workload of learning the culture, their responsibilities, new systems, the people in their organizations, and the task of getting the work done. The learning curve is higher than they thought it was going to be.

In my teenage years, my family was always talking about Russell burning the candle at both ends. I was a little bit crazy, even in high school. My activities exceeded my effectiveness and certain things in my life suffered (primarily my grades). Likewise, there are patterns in people's lives that are often expressed in people's personalities. But this area of change shifts the engagement emphasis as well as adds weight to the role of the conversationalist in terms of protection. Simply asking about the changes that need to be made and what needs to be different carries weight because change is hard, and change often comes with a level of disappointment.

I was listening to a friend who had been part of an organization for over twenty years as the chief operating officer. Over months of consideration and exploring different possibilities, he was sensing a new season approaching. Ultimately, he was feeling he was to take a step of faith to move more into a CEO role in a new organization. After he went through a healthy process of resignation and was honored for his time and commitment, he had a period of rest before he re-engaged with his new work. During that time, he experienced grief for making a change he knew was right.

As a conversationalist, you may find discussion complicated, because on the one hand the person is excited about the new possibilities of what's ahead, and yet they are still holding onto what they have valued from their past. Let me encourage you from my experience that you must be patient. In addition, a high degree of discernment is required to have a sense of what is happening in that person's life as they are making those changes. Are they ready to let go of what's behind, or are they charging ahead into new possibilities and more responsibility without letting go? As we mature and become more rooted in the routine of life, change becomes harder. Yet, conversationally speaking, we are helping people count the cost in order to get ready for their commitment.

Question #7: What Will You Do?

It's decision time. Your heart and mind are so full after exploring and discovering all the possibilities and scenarios, your problem is defined, you're clear as to what has got you to this point, and now you know the path before you. You've counted the cost. You're ready for a change. Now you've got to make a decision. We are at the line of consideration and catalytic. There is a change that is going to have an impact on your life, and at no other point in the conversation (and the relationship) has the need for courage to step forward been so great.

The inspiration for the conversationalist charges us to "consider how we may spur one another on toward love and good deeds" (Hebrews 10:24). The impact of this decision will ultimately come at the benefit of others. It's a short-term pain for a long-term gain. We need the push. We need to be spurred on in order to make a commitment toward action. The bigger the opportunity that is ahead of us, the more courage that is required.

Whenever there is a need for courage, it reveals that we are at the heart of the matter. The defining point of a decision, as well as the defining point of the relationship, is to be able to speak life, belief, and courage into a person in a way that moves them forward. When I first got into life coaching, I spent some time with Dr. John Townsend, from whom I learned many things, one of which was the discipline of paraphrasing. It's the craft of being able to take what you've heard and being able to distill and summarize the details into a statement repeated back to that person. As Dr. Townsend modeled many times for me, he said, "Let me see if I understand this correctly . . . " and then he would go recapping everything I had just shared. When I heard it back from him, there was a clarity that gave me a perspective that I didn't have before.

In addition, paraphrasing allows a person to hear it with fresh ears from somebody else. If any details were missing from your narrative, they could be added in to make the decision clearer for you. If something you said because you felt an emotional weight factored into your decision, then when it has been repeated back to you, you are able to see it more objectively. Ultimately, we are driving toward clarity, which helps us engage in our decisions.

While listening to somebody go on and on about their current situation, we often initially feel an empathy toward them, but when that same person comes back to us repeatedly over the same drama and has yet to really take action on it, it gives us a strong indication that they are really not at a point where they are ready to make a decision. This creates a defining moment for us as conversationalists in terms of our role: Are we moving them forward into a decision of engagement that is actually going to bring about life change, or are we going to stay in a place of empathy and simply become a therapist?

I'm not demeaning prolonged therapy by any means. Some pain runs deep and needs time for healing. This conversational pathway that moves from empathy to engagement can happen in one conversation or it could be spread out over months or years, but either way the conversation (and thus the relationship) is continually moving forward. What will you do? It's the moment of a decision. It's the commitment to change and a declaration to make a difference. You will be a witness to the life-changing moment.

Getting To the Heart of Decision

As you move people along on the conversational continuum from empathy to engagement, there's not a right or wrong answer to any one of the above questions. These seven questions are here to provide a grounding point for where you are in the conversation and to help guide you to the next step. In addition, these questions also give you an ability to gauge how deep you can go in that relationship, as well as an understanding of what that person's capacity is for the relationship. That's the beauty of the conversationalist.

Your job is to actually help people in a discovery process of drawing out of the depths of their lives. Again, Proverbs 20:5 reminds us that "the purposes of a person's heart are deep waters, but one who has insight draws them out." Understanding starts by knowing the questions to ask that will draw out the deep waters of that person's life, and just because the question is asked and they don't have an answer in that moment doesn't mean it is not of value. There are many times I have experienced people coming back months, if not years, later, saying, "I remember when you asked me that question and I went home and talked to my spouse about it," or, "I talked with a few friends and got their feedback."

Truth be told, you really have no idea what is happening on the other end of those questions.

One of the greatest ways you can make preparations in your own heart to be a conversationalist is to lay down your own agenda. Let go of some of your expectations and discipline yourself to not give quick fixes or easy solutions or to respond in trite platitudes that take someone else's deepest concern and trivialize them. The heart of the conversationalist recognizes that there are deep waters in that person's life, and we want to take the time to ask the questions that are meaningful and engaging. The result of such an engagement has the potential for lasting impact, as well as the potential for a friendship that could last a lifetime. That's the heart of the conversationalist.

INSIGHTS AND ACTIONS

1. Where's your comfort level on the continuum? Is it more along the lines of empathy or engagement?
2. Who inspires you at being the best version of yourself? How does that make you feel?
3. The seven questions on the continuum are designed for general use in order to illustrate the progression. What questions would you use to reflect your style and approach? Role-play a conversation with your conversationalist partner.

    1. How are you?
    2. What's going on?
    3. What's the problem?
    4. What are the possibilities?
    5. What's the potential?
    6. What needs to be different?
    7. What will you do?

Chapter 7

LIFE-GIVING RESPONSE

Sitting with a young couple during a halftime show, we caught up for a few minutes and continued through nearly the rest of the game. Something caught my ear when I heard that they were beginning to dream again. His entrepreneurial spirit and her passion for hospitality were coming to the surface when they whispered the word "ranch," a place to come for families experiencing a "inflection point."

This young couple had moved to a new city only eighteen months before, settling into a new home, community, and work. But they sensed something bigger was on the horizon for their family. As their desires and dreams were stirring for a ministry to families, they hoped theirs would continue to grow as well. Their son was turning five, and they wanted another child. The infertility treatments were not working, so they were considering adoption. The approach of time felt like it threatened their hopes. As with any dream, it was tender, and so I prayed I would have the words to respond with an equal sincerity to the gift of their story.

The heart of the conversationalist is so critically important because what stirs your heart helps you spur on the people you are listening to. It is important to be able to take the time to consider what's happening in their life, and to listen to their story with discernment, wisdom, and understanding, then gracefully respond with, "I believe in you! I'm looking forward to the day when I see the expression of these dreams become a reality. We are going to celebrate it."

We have covered a lot of ground so far in this book about preparing the heart to engage as a listener, which will help us interact in a deeper and more meaningful way with the relationships in our life. Now we need to consider how we are going to respond to what is shared. Considering this serves as a transition point as we move into the questions of the conversationalist. So far in the conversation, we have done a lot of asking and listening, but at some point a response is required. And it's this response that may help us transition into the specific life-changing questions.

Think for a moment of those people who have inspired you the most—where something in their story caused your heart to beat a little faster, even caused your hands to sweat and your countenance to shift. You are simply responding at a heart level to something that may have connected with your story. There's something in what's being shared that moves us and stirs our hearts, which demands a response from us.

As conversationalists, we have the opportunity to see such moments to capture the essence of what we are thinking and feeling. The gift of such a response may be the thing that spurs that person on to the work they were just sharing about. If someone is giving you a treasure that's been unlocked from the vault of their heart, then you need to respond in kind by giving a life-giving response.

What Is a Life-Giving Response?

If the discovery process is moving from empathy to engagement, then your response may include the themes of energy, experience, and encouragement. These three themes provide a grid of discernment for you to think through what is happening at a heart level. As I have reflected on hundreds of conversations in which I have been invited into sacred moments where someone has shared the heart of what matters most to them, I have responded by at least one these themes, whether through a statement, a story, or by a written response. This is my response to what stirs their heart as they have taken the time to consider the love and good deeds they want reflected in and through their life.

A response worthy of the person sharing deserves more than quick platitudes and cliché statements. Their sharing a specific story demands a specific response from us, more than "I don't know what to say," or "That sounds amazing," or "Good luck with that." As you want to mature further in friendship, your response represents the defining moment in the friendship. How will you respond?

Response to Energy

If your work as a conversationalist is primarily to intently engage in listening and asking questions that get to the heart of the matter, then you need to watch and read the response of the person sharing. For my friends who may be challenged in missing the obvious, consider the picture of a dashboard on a car. Depending on the kind of person you are interacting with, this dashboard may vary from an old pickup truck to a new Mercedes. This means that the dashboard of needles versus a digital display simply represents the indicators of what's important to that particular person.

As you are sitting stagnant, there is not a lot going on, yet as you move into traffic or are driving along the open road, conversationally speaking, every question or comment, detail or story, represents miles along the road or intersections for turning points in the discussion. Where you are going is important, but you, as a conversationalist, can keep your eye on the dashboard for what moves the needle.

The energy that is required to run a vehicle is like the energy that stirs the heart of a person. That is to say, as you listen to where the conversation is going you can also get an indication of what's most important by the energy that is being talked about and shared. Again, what stirs the heart is an indication to what spurs on to love and good works. Your response is correlated by making observations to what's getting the most energy in that person's life.

As a listener, you are paying attention to the details that matter most to the other person, but at the same time you are paying attention to their response to those details. You might say this is easier to read for those who are more expressive in their responses versus those who are more even-keeled and less expressive in their sharing, but if you are paying attention you can still get an indication as to where they are giving their greatest energy.

We are listening so we can discern what is going on. Thoughts may range from areas of interest, hobbies, or daily activities—programs happening at church, activities with the kids, or even business opportunities that are being explored. They may often be expressed at stress points in difficult circumstances or in relationships, but if you listen to the details, there are words, phrases, or expressions that reveal values and priorities. This is a critically important response because as you are listening you're also observing where the person's energies, efforts, and strengths are being aligned to what matters most in their lives.

One of the greatest values of observation and discernment is simply bringing into focus a new perspective that listens and observes the consistencies and the inconsistencies in that individual's life. More often than not, by simply restating what you have heard in regard to their energy, you can affirm the consistencies where they're aligned to such efforts, while at the same time acknowledging any disconnects. It's a response of understanding that may invoke a healthy change in the person's life. Such an observation of a person's energy leads us to the next point of experience.

An Experiential Response

This second theme of response has to do with two facets of observation. First is the experience of watching someone's life. The more history you have with someone, the more details you have to point to as a reference. You'll know whether what they are saying to you actually aligns with other events in their life.

Your experience of observation over longer periods of time is affirming and validating. When you come alongside someone and say, "I have been watching your life. These are the details I see and the memories that stand out to me," that is one of the greatest gifts you can offer because you have become a witness to their life. This can come by watching someone over a lifetime or simply by paying attention to just a few comments or questions. They are watching the graceful manner in which you dealt with a difficult situation or acknowledged the grace that was still needed. You are responding with a certain level of empathy to pain or difficulty, as well as acknowledging areas where they have taken action and engaged. You are celebrating those experiences.

The second part of experience is your personal response or how you were impacted during those moments. It's one thing to acknowledge what you saw in his or her life, but it is something else to take it to another level of what you felt and how you were moved by that person's story and actions. It is your opportunity to express how you are inspired by this person. This may be one of the easiest responses, even if you feel overwhelmed by someone's story and his or her desire to go do something that is extraordinary. When you put words to what you feel, it is an affirmation, but it also serves the person by helping them understand the impact of his or her story as well.

When people share their life with us, it's often heartfelt and they know they need to do something about it, but they're not even sure where to focus or how to take the next step. Your response of how you have personally been impacted in specific ways gives focus to how to best steward their energy and experience moving forward. This leads us to the third theme of response, which is encouragement.

A Response of Encouragement

To encourage is to impart courage. Encouragement always has to do with the heart. It's at this place of response to someone's life where we consider how to spur them on toward love and good deeds. Encouraging them acknowledges that the world needs their gift. Encouraging will have an impact on other people's lives—just by listening in this moment or over a weekend or a lifetime, you are encouraging them that they have a gift that needs to be clarified, developed, and released in a specific way.

It's courage that says, "You can do this. I believe in you. Go for it. I am with you." But it's also encouragement that comes in a specific way by acknowledging the gifts, the competency, and the character of those people. It's acknowledging the strengths in their life and how you see those abilities impacting their world. It's also acknowledging what you see in them in a specific way that may refer to their background, their family, the community where they were raised, their schooling or the training experiences they have had, the church that they have been a part of, or the circles of friends they belong to. It's the response to their life in full and a holistic sense of what you see and observe.

Encouragement is that moment of looking someone in the eye and saying, "I've considered your life and I am looking forward to learning more. But today, for what I understand, see, and feel, when you apply your energy in these areas, I see it making an impact in other people's lives. I see it brings out the best in you. You have a joy and a sense of fulfillment in your life. When you align these activities with your abilities, somehow God blesses them and I am inspired. I just want to encourage you that whatever the pathway is, whatever decisions need to be made, whatever part I have to play, I love this side of you and I want to see more of it."

Watch Your Language

As you walk through the response of someone's life using one or all of these—energy, experience, and encouragement—you'll want to bring these together with the tool of language. Language is an important part of any culture, whether it's in another country or in a community of people who reflect your values and way of life. When you can listen as a conversationalist to the language that's being used, and then adapt your response of understanding and discernment by bringing in that language, you will lower some of the barriers for others to receive feedback and encouragement from you.

Words really do mean something. So, as you offer a new perspective, insight, or observation about a person's life, and you use those words that connect with them the most, it allows your message to be received and embraced with greater levels of sincerity and less distraction. Such language and words most often come from listening intently to the details of those stories, especially the ones that seem to be closest to the heart. Such details also serve to add weight, not only to our observations but also to further questions.

As we move further into dialogue as conversationalists, we will notice more general theme-based questions move to greater levels of specificity. Our discernment and ability to respond with greater clarity is a gift that really is rare, and our response to someone's life may be the catalyst that ignites a fire for change. These three thematic responses serve as a guide to move from general affirmation to a more specific, mature response to the life that's just been shared with you. As you grow in this place of maturity, it leaves room for another possible response. While it is not necessarily true for all my conversations and relationships, it's something I have noticed as a possibility. It's the response of a dream.

Imagine for a Moment . . .

You have laid the foundation of consideration, which is the discipline of a reflective yet specific response to what energizes an individual's life, what experiences reflect those energies, and you have encouraged them. The response of a dream comes when the time and setting are right. It usually starts with "I can imagine if . . ." As they are faithful to steward these gifts and the passion in your heart, your impact will only continue to grow, resulting in changed lives. It's letting your imagination create a picture of a person's life that may be so much fuller than they can imagine in the present.

Your gift of perspective invites possibilities for their future that they can't yet see for themselves. They may have the greatest ideas in the world, but it's impossible for a person to know how they are experienced by another. If you walk alongside them and relay how you are truly blessed by experiencing their life alongside them, you're blessing them in a way that will mature and grow the possibilities of that dream becoming a reality. It's the gift of a dream that's rarely ever given and it may start with you.

What you are doing is declaring a future for somebody by painting a picture. You are opening the perspective of their world to greater possibilities than they have ever considered or imagined. For those who may have lost hope, are stuck, or may have experienced a deep disappointment, a dream is a gift. The vision for someone's life begins the process for them discovering a vision for themselves.

You are painting a picture inviting someone's interpretation of what a new reality can become for him or her. For those who would see this process as too predictive and representing a risk to the relationship, I would say they are right. It is a risk. But isn't the work of a conversationalist a risk? Isn't even asking a single meaningful question a risk? Doesn't working at a heart level leave us somewhat vulnerable? Such an exercise presents not only a picture but also a possible map for them to begin taking steps into that reality. Your role as a conversationalist is to guide rather than demand or dictate. It is their journey, and your role is to encourage them along the way. If such a picture serves to get them moving, then you have done your job well.

For those who would call such an exercise prophesying, let's be clear that prophesying is simply truth telling. Your role as a conversationalist is bringing truth to bear, shedding light on the dark places that may have been shadowed, and presenting truth in a graceful, loving way that helps provide perspective. The apostle Paul instructs us in 1 Corinthians 14 that we are to desire the prophetic gift, which is for the purpose of comfort, strength, and encouragement. I do not know anyone who does not want these three in his or her life.

Painting a picture of someone else's future may come from a short-term intuition, but more often than not it comes from walking alongside a person and being a witness to their life. Your commitment of time allows you insight that is only reserved for a precious few.

Pray for Wisdom, Insight, and Understanding

Every engagement should be done in a prayerful response, so that you'll be able to respond with understanding, insight, and discernment. James 1:5 says, "If any of you lacks wisdom, you should ask God, who gives generously to all without finding fault, and it will be given to you." Wisdom is a free gift from God, which means that new insights, understanding, and discernment is only a prayer away. I can tell you beyond a shadow of a doubt that as you pray for the people you are in conversations with, God is faithful to give you insights that are needed to help guide you as a conversationalist, even giving you the right questions to ask.

When you consider the work of the conversationalist, the heart must precede the questions. As you pray for those you love, not only will God give you wisdom but he will prepare your heart to be an extension of his love and grace, as well as a way to express truth. Paul prays for the church in Ephesians, that they would be filled with the Spirit of wisdom and revelation, and that they would be grounded in God's love. As you mature in your role of conversationalist, you will find your heart stirred in deeper ways, and such a stirring is the very thing that will spur others on toward love and good deeds.

> The heart must precede the questions.

For the young couple sharing their dream, they gave me the privilege to dream with them. Prayerful listening opened the door for a life-giving response. Their story stirred my heart; their tears drew some of my own, and so I responded to their zeal and energy by sharing a few points of affirmations and even changes in their commitment to consider. I responded how I was moved by their story, and I also shared how my time of being with them made me feel. I encouraged them, specifically calling out their gifts, strengths, and passion, and I shared some consideration for next steps to confirm their direction.

It was the Holy Spirit who provided these insights, which were a gift of wisdom in that moment. What an inspiration that, in a small way, will be defining for them. I'm confident it will spur them on toward their dream of love and good deeds—I am certainly spurred on by their story. I look forward to the day of seeing their future children, whether biological or adopted, sitting on the "ranch," seeing other families bonded and launched beyond their "inflection points" to a great impact. What a day that will be.

INSIGHTS AND ACTIONS

1. How would you respond to the young couple presented at the beginning of this chapter?

2. Consider ways you could be more intentional with a life-giving response:

   a. Responding to their energy (reading their physical responses)

   b. Responding to their experience

   c. Responding with words of encouragement

3. Has anyone ever shared with you a dream for their life? If their life-giving response resonated with you, how did that make you feel? What would keep you from doing the same for someone else?

4. Take time to encourage and affirm your conversationalist partner. Describe the character, strengths, and positive choices you see today as well as what can be in the future.

SECTION TWO

The Questions of the Conversationalist

The questions we ask in conversation are the doorway to meaningful places in relationships. Those who ask good questions and encourage honest responses will discover a growing depth of conversational exchange.

At the end of each chapter are key questions of the conversationalist. But before asking others these questions, start by answering them for yourself. You'll be surprised at what you discover about yourself, which will provide the perspective and confidence to ask these questions of others.

Chapter 8

Passion: What Difference Do You Hope to Make?

We had the privilege of hosting Kelsey in our home for dinner. She is a young lady in her early twenties, just finishing college, working part-time, and sorting through the questions of what to do next with her life. The dinner had been scheduled for a few weeks, so there was a bit of anticipation for our time together. Cari made a wonderful meal that made me want to slow down and enjoy every bite.

It had been a full day for all of us, and we had lots of stories to share early into our dinner. We asked a few questions about Kelsey just to catch up on her activities with school, work, and friendships. She was especially excited to share all the details from the first few dates with a young man whom we know. When we asked about her plans after college, she really had no idea where she would go, what she would do, and the future seemed uncertain for her.

Somewhere in the course of our relaxed dinner conversation, it moved from casual conversation into her sharing a few stories that represented some areas of disappointment and hurt in her life. As we listened, we could feel a little bit of heartache for her, offering a few comments of comfort and care. Then Kelsey moved the conversation from the low point of heartache to one of hope and excitement. We could see the transformation on her face—from sadness to a bright countenance.

She said, "I have something that I have been dreaming about, but I really haven't shared it with many people. I've been dreaming about making a magazine for young people. It would be gritty and real and beautiful. It would have pages and binding that are quality and heavy to touch, so that readers can feel the book just as much as they read it." She went on to share for the next forty-five minutes about all the details of this magazine, the images and the stories she wanted within it, the team that was coming together to help make it a reality, and when she hopes to have it released for a first printing. We love Kelsey's story; it was a privilege to be able to listen to an early dream that will one day become a reality.

Passion is a life-changing subject that deeply scratches an area of our lives that is so rarely explored and discovered. It is more felt than articulated. And, frankly, the area of passion can be a little overwhelming for some. To take something that you feel so deeply about and form thoughts and words that lead you to action is a powerful thing indeed. Passion is more than an area of interest, like something you'd see on the news that would move you beyond concern—passion moves you to action.

For most of us, there are many areas in our lives that move us, but over time we see a narrowing of focus to the few things that really capture our heart and that we want to give our lives to. When first forming the life-changing questions, the area of passion and the difference we wants to make actually begin with our sense of purpose. If I could probe even more you may ask, why are you here? These questions leave most people feeling daunted with the answers, as if to say, "What is the most important thing about me, and how do I want to take that and contribute it to making the world a better place?"

After asking this question hundreds if not thousands of times, what moves the conversation toward a decision is simply asking, "What difference do you hope to make?" It's a question that is attainable by anyone, whether it's my hundred-year-old grandmother or my ten-year-old son. Were you to ask Grady this question, he would say he wants to be a good and godly man, to love people, and to do the right thing. Even at forty something, his dad would aspire to do the same. As we have more life experiences, that answer may narrow to a focus that has a defining and measurable impact on the world around us, starting within our family and close friendships, our neighborhood, the community around us, our church, our workplace, and so on.

As we move into these seven questions, for you to develop conversationally and draw out the answers to these questions for the people in your life, I would encourage you to have a grounding on the answers for yourself before you spend time asking them of others. If you and I were sitting together and I asked you, "What are you passionate about, and what is the difference you hope to make?" how would you answer those questions? We may explore different stories from your past, what the expression of those may look like today, and what that might look like in the future.

This past New Year's Eve, before the ball dropped, some of the announcers threw around whimsical resolutions, hoping for peace and harmony in the world. And yes, wouldn't that be wonderful to see such a resolution become an actual reality? The surface answer to such questions must ultimately come from the heart that stirs you in such a way that it gives focus to your actions and leads to commitment. If I were to sit with you, I might even press you for how it's expressed in the use of your time and **A passion without a plan really only stays a dream.** finances. If we were to be so candid to look at your calendar and your checking account, not from a point of criticism but for context of the expression of what really matters most to you, we could see that where you put your time and money reveals the heart of what matters most to you.

A passion without a plan really only stays a dream. As you begin articulating that dream and taking steps in concrete ways to reach it, such a dream really becomes a reality. We live in a day and age where the issues of social justice and the motivation to do something about those issues has captured the hearts of young people around the world. It is really quite inspiring to sit and listen to the dreams and passions of young people, of what they hope to do with their lives so they can make a difference in the world in which they live. And often, as is the case with younger people, they lack the resources or the experience to really make that dream become a reality.

Yet, by asking about those dreams, it spurs you on, inspires you, and gives you context that the resources, experiences, and relationships you have may help ignite those dreams for that young person and accelerate them to a reality. In addition, it stirs your heart for a passion that maybe has plateaued, been buried, or been lost.

When you engage with that question, the depth, sincerity, and possibilities have a far greater potential if you have actually wrestled these questions, defining some of the answers, and committing your life to them. As I have engaged in so many of these conversations regarding this question, when we actually get below the surface to some of the details and circumstances around a person's passions, more often than not we hit the wall of disappointment or regret. Whether as a teenager, young adult, or someone in the prime of their life, that person's dream and the expression of their passion had a different reality. Life now looks different from what they expected. Oftentimes, those unmet expectations kept them from re-engaging with what they were most passionate about. If you struggle with answering these questions for yourself, know that there is a reason—these questions may be difficult to answer on your own, which is why we need conversationalists who will help draw out the depths of such answers.

Why is this so hard, and why is it so important? It is because passion intersects with our story. One definition for our life purpose may be when our passion meets the world's need. The idea of exploring what we truly love to do and what we spend our time investing in intersecting with the needs of those around us is truly the indication of why we are here. And as we mature in our thinking and the experiences around our passion intersect with the world's needs, it gives us a greater sense of clarity and conviction to move forward into our calling.

Attempting to define your passion can be daunting because it intersects with your story. And more often than not, the highs and lows, and the bends and turns of your story have their moments of disappointment, hurt, and heartache. I am not a psychologist, but I've learned as I have spent time with enough people in trusted, confidential conversations that when we hit a point of full expression of their passion—what they want to do with their lives and the difference they hope to make—I am only a question or two away from revealing why that is such a motivation in their life.

A counselor friend of mine often says that people are either motivated by priority or pain. Not every passion is entirely motivated by pain; it simply could be a deep conviction or an inward sense of your highest value—what you want to give your life to— yet somewhere in the psychology of it all, the question remains: What breaks your heart? When you see something that stirs you so deeply that you may not even be able to put words to it, this gives a good indication of a focus point of your passion. It may not need to be a vocational career or a full-time commitment; rather, this may be a simple expression of your life within the context of your family and work that you just need to dedicate some of your time and resources to.

The greater the pain from your past, the greater potential impact expressed through your passion.

The greater the pain from your past, the greater potential impact expressed through your passion. It's with such a statement that I want to introduce an idea that truly runs heart-deep for me: one of the highest priorities of my life is a person's redemptive story. Regardless of your faith in Christ, once the pain in your life has been healed, it gives expression to those who are struggling with the same pain. As you experience healing, victory, and freedom, you may feel called to walk alongside others still hurting so they may also experience the same liberty. The depths of people's lives are what make the work of the conversationalist so critically important in guiding, exploring, and discovering these expressions.

The redemptive story of people's lives reveals what truly motivates them, spurs them on to have an impact by loving others and helping them define a regular expression of that work, along with the routines and rhythms of their daily life. This journey of discovering your redemptive story and the expression of it really is the process of discovering your life's purpose. And when you have that expression, it gives you energy, focus, and fulfillment in ways that you have never experienced before. Again, it is worthy of repeating: you cannot get there on your own. Your passion at some point must intersect with other people's needs. There will always be a relational engagement to your redemptive story.

The work of the conversationalist guides the discussion from the simple answers of the difference you hope to make to a specific expression that is unique to you. If you haven't already, you need to explore these answers for yourself, looking for specific ways to engage your passion. As you engage as a conversationalist, drawing out the same answers for others, you will find it considerable if not catalytic, resulting in a life change of something others have always known but never really explored or fully experienced before. Then as your conversation matures and develops, that purpose will develop into a plan, which will be tested by the priorities of your life.

As you move forward conversationally, from one to multiple conversations, you can identify the gap of where you are today and where you hope to be in the future, which is the full expression of your passion and the difference you hope to make in the world. One of the greatest joys of a conversationalist is seeing that gap narrow to a full expression of the difference you want to make, making that dream become a reality.

The expression of these ideas is so personal and unique to the individual you are spending time with. It's the entrepreneur hoping to launch that new business. It is the teenagers who hope to see the homeless fed or young people learn how to read to keep them from a life of prison by illiteracy. It's that single person who hopes to find the person they love and raise a family one day. It's that person so full of faith that they hope to see their friends and family in capture that same heart of faith that one day may change the world.

What is your passion and what is the difference you hope to make in this world? Your work as a conversationalist begins by answering that question for yourself, and as you do, engage in dialogue with those in your life, exploring and discovering those answers together. Answering this question will help you find full expression of those passions that will one day intersect with the world's greatest needs—much like my friend Kelsey. Hopefully, one day you will be able to read her magazine, whatever it looks like—the full expression of its color, texture, and the inspiring stories within—but equally inspiring would be seeing that heartfelt dream become a reality.

My friends in Ireland had a dream to showcase their Irish roots and the story of Ireland through photography and cooking, so they brought it all together in a cookbook that could be shared with people in Ireland as well as the United States. Now, many years later, their warmth and wonder has found expression in thousands of homes and at many dinner tables. And it all began with a whispered conversation in an Irish pub so many years ago.

A few weeks ago, a woman in her late forties approached me privately and tearfully after a workshop and said, "Russell, I used to know the answers to these questions. And now I've lost them. After hearing your heart and challenge for me to explore my own answers, I know I need to rediscover what my passions are for today."

This is your assignment: to discover and document your passions—the difference you want to make in our world. I encourage you to answer the questions below for yourself, discuss them with your conversationalist partner, and then ask of another person in your life.

INSIGHTS AND ACTIONS

1. Write down at least ten things you are passionate about. (What makes your heart come alive?)

2. What is the brokenness you see in the world that you have the most compassion for? Where does your passion intersect with the world's need?

3. What is something in your past that you have overcome that now gives you the position to serve and encourage others in that same area?

4. To what degree is your primary work in line with your passions? What could be done to bring your passion and work more in alignment?

5. What dream did you used to have that was met with regret or disappointment? How might that dream have a different expression today?

6. What dream has been dormant that you need to make a plan for?

7. Since a passion without a plan will stay a dream, what one passion will you commit to develop into a plan that will make a difference in someone's life? Discuss this with your conversationalist partner this week.

8. Who will you ask about his or her passions this week? Which question below would be most appropriate for your relationship with this person?

   - What do you like to do with your free time?
   - What makes your heart come alive?
   - If money were no object, what would you do with your life?
   - Other: _____

Chapter 9

Strengths:
What Energizes Your Life?

A few years ago I started meeting with Pete, a local businessman who had about twenty-five employees. He had a solid reputation in the community. His life was marked by great friendships and an extraordinary family, who had overcome sickness and experienced the joy of adopting all of their children. Pete exhibits an energy that is in the top 1 percent of people you meet. He has an enthusiasm for life that is contagious, and somehow he, in just a few minutes and regardless of what you are talking about, spurs you on to go and apply an equal level of passion and engagement to whatever you put your hands to.

Yet those closest to Pete could see the effects of the weariness of travel and the responsibilities of running a company while caring for his family's needs. Underneath his passion and enthusiasm for life, family, and work, the effects of fatigue were beginning to wear him down. Pete is one of those rare and wonderful leaders who truly has a gift of clear vision, for both his personal life and his organization. It's that vision that he consistently communicates, and those in his life are inspired by that vision. He knows where he is headed and why he is headed there. In fact, he has been faithful for over a decade to that sense of mission and purpose expressed through his passion. So what was the problem?

Certainly, the effects of the economic downturn weighed on him, as did contracts with key clients that changed unexpectedly, cash flow challenges, and the difficulties closer to home of a medical nature that were really out of his control. Pete knew that to sustain his direction and a faithfulness to what he was passionate about, he was going to have to change something in his life.

It's at the heart of this discovery dialogue that we would ask, "What is your strength and what energizes your life?" Having a clear sense of your passion and purpose is critically important for the direction of where to apply your energy. Even though you may feel the inspiration that motivates you and therefore moves you in that particular direction, it may not sustain you for the long term. If you were to look at your life's purpose and passion, as well as the priorities that align all of your efforts, we would be looking at the engine of your life. The question of strength and energy is, what fuels your engine?

A more appropriate example may be our own bodies. If we fuel our bodies with healthy food, water, and other natural supplements, those are life-giving and we would feel their effects in our bodies. Yet when we feed our body with junk, we may get a momentary satisfaction from that food, but it's fleeting. Within a short period of time, our energy level, our focus, and our overall performance will begin to waver. If passion is what makes your heart come alive, then strength is what keeps it beating.

> If passion is what makes your heart come alive, then strength is what keeps it beating.

On the subject of strength and energizing activities, books have been written, courses taught, and conferences led—there is no shortage of information, opinions, and philosophies about this idea. For the purpose of the conversationalist, however, we are inviting a dialogue to look at the practical elements of our daily life and discover the energizing activities that, when we do them, we come away with more energy than we had when we started.

My friend David Jewitt, who leads Your One Degree, has spent over two decades with thousands of people around the globe talking about this very subject: "What are your natural God-given drivers?" He helps people look through a list of over three hundred verbs that represent actions and activities, leading them through a simple discovery process of identifying their greens, yellows, and reds, using the imagery of a traffic light.

The reds represent the areas of exhaustion, that, when engaged in, drain us. Yellows are the areas that are neutral, which many of us do because we have to; they neither add to or withdraw from our energy levels. Yet the sum of the yellows is a net negative. The combined total of yellows drains us in the most subtle of ways, constantly eroding away. The greens are the activities we engage in that give us life. Whether we identify ten or twenty-five greens, our discovery process narrows our focus to what gives us energy. We have only two or three driving activities that, when we do them, allows us to give our best. This is especially true for leaders to identify, so that in time and maturity they can delegate many of the yellows and certainly the reds.

This issue is critically important because of the amount of burnout we see in people today. People are doing too much of the wrong things for prolonged periods of time, for months if not years on end, which leads to a fatigue and a depletion of their energy. When energy is low, this results in prolonged periods of discouragement, disillusionment, doubt, and even depression. This issue takes even the best of men and women and puts them on the sidelines of life.

There is a host of issues that affect our energy level and that need to be taken into consideration, yet simple questions remain: What energizes our life? Where do we find strength? What are the things we do that make us feel more alive? As a conversationalist, we have to answer that for ourselves in the simplest and most practical terms. We can actually take time today by beginning to activate those things that bring us strength.

As a conversationalist, I have spent time in hundreds of conversations that, whether in a mentoring context with young leaders or in a coaching context with executives, I see the glaze in their eye as they share all the things on their to-do list, expressing all the responsibilities they have and the burden they feel for how they are going to get them all done. There is a sense of hopelessness that comes up, because it seems too daunting. Then I ask the simplest of questions: "When was the last time you read a good book? When have you hung out with a good friend? When was the last time you exercised? When was the last time you sat and wrote? When was the last time you created something from scratch? When was the last time you helped a friend in need?"

These questions seem so simple on the surface, yet each one of these, representing energizing activities, are like rocket fuel for the engine of your life. These questions are simple but represent a profound reality. Like my friend Pete, we have to do things that give us daily energy, things that, while doing them, actually strengthen us. In some ways, it almost sounds counterintuitive because everything requires energy, but the difference is how we respond when we do them. Do we feel depleted, withdrawn, and fatigued for no apparent reason? Or do we actually feel fully energized? Some of these rhythms and disciplines are engaged in privately, while others are right in the swing of the fullness of our work life.

During many of my mentoring and coaching conversations, when there is an awareness or discovery to people's unique drivers, I see in their countenance the elation of the acknowledgement, let alone the permission, to be able to do the things that give them energy. So I ask this question, "Do you feel selfish when you do these things?" And 90 percent of the time the answer is yes. I don't pretend to understand the psychology of this response, other than that most people feel that it is too good to be true. If they do what they really love to do, and they do it in a way that actually energizes their life, then there must be something wrong with that. It sounds too good to be true, yet for the person who has been committed to a sense of missional purpose for their life for a long period of time, they know the effects of deep fatigue and burnout.

This discussion does not abdicate you from responsibilities that need to get done; rather, it is recognizing your daily rhythms of how you are spending your time. If you're spending most of your day doing things that drain you, then you won't be able to sustain that pace without prolonged effects if something is not quickly changed. This is life-changing when you get to the heart. The root of this issue runs far deeper than self-help thinking. This one conversation is what ultimately led me to make a career change that came at a financial expense, with significant patience and grace exhibited from my family in the transition.

During my personal discovery process and answering these questions, I came to a conviction that my life was energized by activating and influencing others. The connection with people brought me joy as I had the opportunity to communicate ideas that helped inspire people in their life, leadership, and legacy.

One day, as I was working through these ideas, Dave asked me, "Think about sharing your message within the four walls of a building. Then I want you to think about that same group of people and that same message shared in an outdoor setting somewhere in the Rocky Mountains sitting by a campfire. What do you think is going to have a greater impact?"

I smiled back and said, "Are kidding me? I need to be outside."

Then he pressed further, "Why would that have more impact?"

It seemed so obvious to me in that moment, so I said, "Because my heart would be more alive. You're always going to get the best of me when I am outside in creation. Something makes my spirit soar when I am in the beauty of creation."

Then he said, "You need to do that." And I gave him a look that said it was too good to be true. I didn't go sell everything and join a camp, yet prayerfully, with counsel over months, the path became much clearer for me. Eighteen months later, I moved from the back of a warehouse, operating and managing a business that felt more like it was managing me, to the space of coaching CEOs and facilitating executive teams.

When I tell that story, people often ask, "How in the world did you make that transition?" First and foremost, my wife and I prayed a lot. I sought the counsel of those I trusted, of those who could speak into my life and show me things about myself, helping me see in my blind spots. Then I began taking experimental steps in a specific direction, learning with each new opportunity. It was a season of grace in my life and family that, without a doubt, was one of the biggest faith steps we have ever taken.

As you press in beyond news, weather, and sports, and get to the heart of what's happening in people's lives, you may find a theme that those you intentionally choose to engage with are at a transition or inflection point in their life, and they are simply asking, "What do I do with my life?" The further along they are in life, the more experiences they've had, the more resources at their disposal, and the more connections within their network all add up to the opportunities in front of them, which can feel overwhelming. They are daunted by the possibilities, and it puts them at a point of indecision. Your role as a conversationalist is to draw out the answers as to where they find strength and what energizes their life. As they find more of their days filled with those activities, they begin to find fulfillment, satisfaction, and joy to everything they do.

Where Do You Find Joy?

Another access point to find answers to this question is around the attribute of joy. We've discussed the prolonged effects of doing things that drain you and leave you in a state of fog, where you may not be able to find your way through. But another common effect of this state is a loss of joy. If you are in this space, talking about where one finds joy, then you are at the heart of that individual. Pray as you talk, and think well about your words, for there is a time to relate and empathize with a similar story from your life, but more importantly this is your time to listen, not to suggest, prescribe, or give anecdotes—but to simply listen. Your responses may be, "How did that feel? Tell me more. What happened next?"

When you are listening intently at this level, you are letting the soul breathe where it may have felt suffocated before. More often than not, the gift of someone listening in this space leads to someone's personal discovery of things you may not have the history to even ask about in order to draw out. When you are in the space of joy, it has a wonderful way of bringing up history where you as the listener are learning things about this individual that you never even knew. Somehow a rediscovery of a story—a family experience, time with friends, a business experience, a trip to the mission field, a service project, a conversation long forgotten—is a reminder of a time that may be sad for that person, but you may soon see a smile that follows shortly thereafter.

I've seen this dozens of times, when people are reminded of what brought so much joy and satisfaction to their lives. This so often is the key to their discovery process. And somehow in their responsibilities of the day they feel like they have lost a little bit of who they are, and their story reminds them when they had a zeal for life that isn't present today. Depending on the time you have and the setting for your engagement, there may be another discovery that happens and turns the conversation from nostalgia to a realization of what is stealing their joy, what's robbing their strength, and what's taking their energy. This is a turning point of discovery, where they realize this issue has been carrying a weight, and they had no idea the burden it represented. In the fresh air of the space of their soul, they simply say no more. Where you find your joy in life is actually the power source of your strength.

> Where you find your joy in life is actually the power source of your strength.

Define Your Tax

Taxes are the stress points in your life that lead to struggles that strain you, stretch you, and, if you let them linger for too long, compromise your strength. Similar to energizing activities, you have to be aware of where you are putting your strength. When you give your strength to something, do you come away fulfilled or depleted? You have to manage your drivers, and so you need to manage your tax. Where are the stress points in your life?

I have observed that our tax takes more out of us than we realize. I get the privilege of interacting with some of the most amazing people on a regular basis—their strength, the impact of their influence, and their sense of responsibility, loyalty, and good character help them persevere and stay the course when things get hard. Yet the tax they feel and how it influences them from the inside out often doesn't get expressed. We've got to identify these areas, and talking about them helps bring them to light and allows us to evaluate the cost it has on our life. How much mental and emotional energy are they costing us? What is the financial cost? How much sleep am I losing over this issue?

As conversationalists, we can take as much liberty as we like to identify as many areas as we need that are a tax for us. But in the most practical sense of a discovery dialogue, identify the stress points in our life and narrow them down to a few that seem to have a repeated pattern. Then it's time to take action to either put boundaries on them, with clear commitments of our time, or to eliminate them altogether.

Blind Spots and Burdens

We need others because of our blind spots. It is nearly impossible for us to self-evaluate the impact of an issue or an individual on our life and what they are costing us in terms of energy. When we live in the repeated cycle of this pattern, it begins to takes on the characteristic of someone who lives crisis to crisis. It's often those people who have a bit of a savior complex toward those they meet.

I am refreshed by the model of Jesus, who would go into towns and not feel the obligation to meet and minister to everyone who had a need. Even Jesus knew his business, his purpose, and why he was there, and he engaged in deep ways with the few he interacted with. And for those he didn't engage with, he modeled by sending out his disciples to go do the same for others. We all have our blind spots, and our role as conversationalists is to dialogue through the tax in the lives of others: "What's stealing your strength, robbing you of our energy, and taking your joy?"

We are letting go of the good in order to grab the great. That is a simple phrase, but it is difficult to navigate. Letting go of good stuff is hard. Letting go of hard stuff is hard too, but at least it is easier than letting go of what is good. A friend of mine recently asked me, "Is it easier to say no today or to say no later when you are more vested and involved along the way?"

This subject is really about discovering the highest and best use of our God-given strength and bringing that energy into our daily life, so that it can be expressed in our closest relationships—the ones involving our family, friends, and fellow professionals. Like my friend Pete, over the course of a year he stayed true to his mission and his passion, significantly changing things along the way. It effected his time, his daily rhythms, and how he interacted with his employees and prospective clients. He had a pattern of overextending his commitments beyond his capabilities, and in his desire to honor those commitments he was getting stretched thinner and thinner. How he fulfilled that mission within his organization absolutely impacted their strategic plans and focus, and those strategies aligned with laser focus to what energized his life. He got a handle on the taxes in his life, which resulted in his even firing a few clients. His energy was renewed for his work and, most importantly, he got his joy back.

As a conversationalist, I got to witness the transformation in Pete's life. It had an impact not only on his business and his family, but also on his health. He has a radical story of losing over a hundred pounds as a personal transformation and outward expression of the inward renewal that took place. As you engage in conversations with people in your life, if they experience that look of fog and fatigue, disillusionment, or even depression, ask them this question, "What energizes your life?" And then take time to guide them through the answer to that question.

INSIGHTS AND ACTIONS

1. Think back to a season of life, a trip, a project, or another opportunity where you felt most alive. What aspects of that time were energizing for you?

2. List at least three activities that energize you (greens), two that are neutral (yellows), and three that steal your strength and take your joy (reds).

3. Look at your calendar and determine how much of your week you spend doing the things that drain you and how much of your week you spend doing those things that give you life.

4. How can you manage your must-do responsibilities in a different way so they are less taxing on your mental, emotional, and physical energy?

5. When is a time you've experienced burnout? What led up to your burnout and what did you do to recover?

6. What changes can you make to incorporate more life-giving activities into your day?

7. What are the things you enjoy so much that you actually feel selfish when you do them? How often do you give yourself permission to do them?

8. Since mission, purpose, and dreams do not keep a person from burnout, what one strength will you commit to exercise more frequently so that you have a sense of greater joy and fulfillment when you do your work? Discuss this with your conversationalist partner this week.

9. Who will you ask about his or her strengths this week? Which question below would be most appropriate for your relationship with this person?
   - What are your strengths?
   - How much of your week is devoted to things that align with your strengths?
   - How do you manage activities that do not necessarily align with your strengths?

Chapter 10

Attitude:
What's the Attitude of Your Heart?

Attitude is everything. And if attitude is not everything, it sure does help. It makes the difference between winning or losing, surviving or thriving, excelling or existing. The thrill of competition between two opponents often leads up to the final score in the last minutes, which leaves one with the thrill of victory and the other with the agony of defeat.

For the victor, it is easy to celebrate the podium, the trophy, and the accolades of their accomplishment, but we don't have to look too far to recognize it wasn't just that individual or team that won the trophy—it was a whole group of people speaking into, coaching, mentoring, and encouraging. Behind the scenes, before the heat of the competition, how many dozens of moments were there when the athlete was tempted to say, "It's too hard. Let's give up"? It's here we see that skills can be developed and that attitude is a choice. It's how you choose to compete and bring the full measure of you and your team into the arena.

Equally, for those who experience defeat, what makes the difference as to whether they choose to compete again? What will help them rise once again, to stand strong, to compete another day? Is it skill? Is it the ability to stay engaged in the midst of opposition, defeat, and discouragement? After five years of watching great victories from my daughter's high school and club volleyball teams, it's a marvel to see how subtle shifts in attitude cause them to work together, so they can come from behind and take the victory. For every player and coach, the key is understanding that it is attitude that truly motivates people to tap into those reserves of strength—to push through the line, to overcome odds, and to finish strong.

Attitude goes well beyond the sports arena—it carries over into every other area of life. And it's these attitudes that set the atmosphere to make ordinary moments extraordinary.

Attitude Reveals the Heart

As a conversationalist engaging in the seven life-changing questions, attitude is by far the easiest to read. For family and close friends, I'm easy to read. When I'm excited about something, everyone will know it, and the opposite is true as well. My disinterest or discouragement shuts down my countenance and brings the dialogue to a quick stop. Some days I really am just tired, but other days I'm wrestling with different issues. As you get to know me, you'll see areas of interest that get my heart stirred and others not so much.

I'm not an angry person, so if I'm under stress I typically shut down. As mentors, coaches, and friends have done for me over the years, they help clarify what's going on in my heart. What emotions are being expressed, and why am I so excited and engaged (or apathetic and disengaged)? More often than not, I don't fully realize the impact of my attitudes on my family, friends, and workplace.

> Once we know how others experience us through our attitudes, then we can begin making a change.

Awareness is half the battle when it comes to having a good attitude. Once we know how others experience us through our attitudes, then we can begin making a change. It's a life-changing conversation, yet it requires courage when our attitude is unhealthy. It also requires encouragement when we see something really special expressed. It's those celebration moments that your heart is fully alive and at work.

In this way, attitude is contagious in both directions. We want to call out the best in people when we see them in their sweet spot. It has more to do with the sincerity than with anything else. If I have a problem with forgetting my deodorant, I hope I have a friend comfortable enough to tell me I stink. The same would be true if my attitude stinks too. If I have a special date night planned for my wife or my girls, then I want to look my best. It feels good when someone notices the extra shine in my shoe or the skip in my step, and I might find myself getting dressed up more often. The same is true with my attitude as well.

Over the years, I've been a part of many Christian groups. In recent years, I have had the opportunity to facilitate many team-building offsites within an organization. Maybe it's more instinct than intuition, but I can get the feel of a room within a few minutes based on a couple comments and the interaction within the team. Navigating a few questions and facilitating interaction gives me a sense of how healthy this team is. The observations of whether they have a good sense of humor or agitation toward the slightest comments, of whether the team engages in good-natured debate and bantering, and of who the players are and the roles they represent on the team lend themselves to the atmosphere in the room. Whether in a team setting, a small group, a family, or even one-on-one, attitude ultimately reflects the atmosphere that either ignites or dampens the conversation. As you find yourself a part of these conversations, or facilitating these conversations, the grounding point for attitude has everything to do with perspective.

By nature, we may have an optimistic attitude. We may find unique ways of looking at the best in any situation and may even challenge ourselves to find the little glimmer of light surrounded by a whole lot of darkness. Even the most gracious and humble can find themselves meeting with people in places and engaged in conversations they don't want to be in, and they're looking for the exit door. Through these difficult moments, what makes the difference in our attitude is our perspective. You may find yourself in one of these places. As you look around your own life, you may see the majority of your engagements and commitments are really great (or at least good). Yet you may find that there are a few areas that are plain hard.

For you to engage with another as a conversationalist, you have to first evaluate your own attitude. What is the attitude of your heart? It is critically important to have your heart healthy and well as you engage as a conversationalist. If you are struggling in your attitude, then it's an indication that there's something at a heart level that needs to be realigned and recalibrated so that it can reveal the root of what you're feeling.

If we were to engage conversationally one-on-one and I were to ask you about your relationship with your boss or a colleague at work who got the promotion when you should have, or about your response to the person who cut you off in the road and revealed some real anger, we would find that there's a reason why those attitudes are there. The discovery process of bringing an awareness of why your attitude and the emotions that get expressed requires some engagement. Oftentimes, the reason our attitudes are left unchecked is because we haven't had people in our life who have taken the time to press beyond the surface of an "off" comment, a roll of the eyes, or a genuine expression of aggression.

Attitude carries more weight than we realize. It's amazing how one look, shrug, or whispered comment can do more to damage than restoration. As we look at how to encourage one another on to love and good deeds, what if we considered the opposite effect? What if we considered what fosters hate and bad works? It's not even fun to think about this, let alone write about it. This kind of negativity expresses itself in selfishness, control, manipulation, and other destructive behaviors. It's the bad side of attitude that does everything but build up others. If there was something coming to mind that may have been dormant or a lingering attitude that you have felt justified in holding onto, then that is contaminating your heart. It has more of an impact on those around you than you realize. In this context, it is limiting you from being a conversationalist.

One of the reasons why I am asked to come in and facilitate teams is often because I have the candor to speak truth in a way that can be received to hopefully eliminate the root of whatever is causing the dysfunction. I have the joy of seeing teams of people go from severe dysfunction to fully functioning, high-performing teams because the root of what's preventing them from coming together in unity was eliminated, thus enabling them to work together in a complementary way instead of from a competing, egotistical, and often self-serving agenda. It's this line of thinking that often gets darkest before the light of day can break through.

Setting the Right Environment

As you grow as a conversationalist, you need to be aware of the environment around you. What's affecting the attitude of the people for good? You have the opportunity that sets the tone and conditions the kind of conversations that will help facilitate a better attitude and take the conversation further than where it has been. As a conversationalist, you can walk into a room and be able to survey the attitudes that are present based on the comments that are being made, whether verbal or nonverbal. Oftentimes, these attitudes simply reflect the culture of the people represented. People often mirror the strongest personality in the room.

I recently met a young man who was in a position to take over the family business. After we met for just a few minutes and talked about the schedule for the day, his rather friendly demeanor seemed to change to one of resistance. Within an hour I was sitting in his office watching an exchange happen between an older father on the edge of retirement with the younger son who was going to be taking over the business. The father's word was still law and the son had to abide by that. The dad had a certain way of doing business, and the son was clearly caught in the tension of trying to honor his father's wishes, yet he wanted to protect himself from the stigma and cynicism that his father carried. In the son's light-hearted way, he was fighting against the culture that represented the family business.

The conversationalist would be wise to discern the forces of strong attitudes, protect his or her heart from being pulled down into the mire of negativity, and look for attitudes that are inspiring and energizing, which can be leveraged for real growth.

Attitude of Gratitude

Regardless of the context, one of the strongest tools we can lever-age is gratitude. What are we thankful for? Such a question can open the heart of the youngest of children to the oldest, and take them places for new insights and understanding, well beyond the defined terms of their immediate circumstance. As conversation-alists, we're inviting them to have a new perspective by having a dialogue where we explore and discover the possibilities of what they are grateful for.

Thankfulness taps into people's hearts to see things in a way they have never seen them before. This helps get the conversation moving forward, even when a team has faced defeat and says, "I am so grateful we even got to this level of competition," and then moves from grati-tude to drawing from the wisdom of experience, which would have been missed if they hadn't gotten to that level. What if we had given up along the way? We would have missed the opportunity to learn, grow, and develop.

> Thankfulness taps into people's hearts to see things in a way they have never seen them before.

It is a joy to have had mentors and coaches in our lives, who have helped give us perspective, who have walked where we have walked, and have cast a vision to our road ahead. These defeats and disappointments were necessary building blocks to prepare us for the victory we may one day see. Attitude is not all about winning or losing; it is about the joy of the journey in between, those we have met, and experiences we have had along the way.

As we move conversationally from this place of inviting a new perspective, engaging an attitude, and drawing from the wisdom of our experiences, we are led to a place of true, genuine contentment. This is not a contentment that leaves us without ambition. We still have a passion and an energy for life that moves toward our purpose, our passion, and our priorities. Contentment recognizes that as we step out—exercising faith, strength, and courage—there has to be something deep within us, a peace on our lives, that grounds us and allows us to operate in a spirit of contentment. Some opportunities that will be met with challenges, and we may be tempted to give up because of potential defeat. It's such contentment that allows us to stay steady and stay the course.

We live in a day and age where people are rewarded primarily for their skills and competency, their ability to produce, their ability to turn a product into something that is profitable and of value. Whether we go to school for education or we develop such skills under the weight of responsibilities, it's the result of the sharpening of these skills as they intersect with the needs around us that we find affirmation, accolades, and compensation for our performance. Yet somehow within this system, we are not rewarded so directly for the development of our character and its expression in our attitude.

Attitude Reflects Character

Your role as a conversationalist may have one of the greatest impacts because you have helped develop others in ways that are not directly rewarded. As you look around the workplace, the reason for so much compromise that is having an effect on government, organizations, and institutions, as well as the church, is simply that people are put in positions of responsibility because of their gifts, yet the weight of responsibility exceeds their character development.

As Christians, we have access to exhibit the personality of the Holy Spirit as described by his fruit from Galatians 5:22–23.

The fruits of the Spirit are love, joy, peace, patience, kindness, goodness, faithfulness, gentleness, and self-control. These traits represent characteristics that can be activated and lived out in full expression in every area of our life, yet so often in our families, friendships, churches, and workplaces, we do not love each other well. We do not exhibit joy from our life. We don't operate from a place of peace, and we lack considerable patience under the day-to-day testing we experience.

Success and defeat in the trials of life have the potential to develop character within us. Yet it's under these conditions where we are tested and the heart of who we are and the attitude that we reflect is revealed. If you really want to get to know a person, then watch how they respond through times of significant difficulty. In addition, if you want to see their true heart, then watch how they respond to success. It's these moments of difficulty that reveal pride and arrogance or a genuine humility. It reveals opinions and agendas that weren't clear in the beginning.

All of these characteristics have the potential to be fully developed and must be done in relational engagement. It's almost as if these characteristics are drawn out from the heart, and recognizing other attributes that may dominate our life and attitudes need to be diminished and removed. So often on the surface, when we take on a subject like attitude, it's one we immediately associate with performance—getting things done and crossing the finish line. It is about the heart, and when it does get tough, that will make the difference and help us get across the finish line.

Yet more than an event or even an experience, attitude reflects itself in a disciplined life where such disciplines form habits. And those habits form character. The result of this character formation ultimately develops a reputation. Which of these characteristics do you want to see developed to the fullest? When you consider how people experience you, which of these characteristics would you want to have spoken over you? This is a wonderful discovery that, as you engage as a conversationalist, will take you to places of renewed perspective, gratitude, and thanksgiving. Contentment settles your life and acts as a foundation that truly is life-changing.

INSIGHTS AND ACTIONS

1. Describe a coach, teacher, or boss whose attitude inspired you to keep going during a significant challenge. What was the impact?

2. How do you think others around you would describe your attitude? How would you describe your attitude?

3. How much are you reflecting the attitudes of people at work or home, for good or bad? What is the effect of their attitudes on you?

4. What toxic attitudes are you exposed to on a regular basis? What are you doing to protect yourself from its negativity?

5. List twenty-five things you are thankful for today.

6. How can your family or team express gratitude to change their attitudes?

7. Since attitude is contagious in both directions, what one attitude (or fruit of the Spirit) do you want to cultivate and practice this month? Discuss this with your conversationalist partner this week.

8. Who will you ask about his or her attitudes this week? Which question below would be most appropriate for your relationship with this person?

   - When have you been tempted to give up?

   - What has helped you try again after disappointment or defeat?

   - How do you protect against toxic attitudes in your relationships?

   - Other: _____

Chapter 11

STEWARDSHIP: WHAT'S BEEN ENTRUSTED TO YOUR CARE?

The end of 2001 (specifically, September 11) was marked by significant events that awakened a fear and a vulnerability our country had never experienced before. This began a war on terrorism abroad as well as at home, bringing in security measures at our borders and airports, and it put the United States on high alert to the threat of another attack. The economic impacts on the United States were globally felt.

Running an office furniture business in the hotbed of Atlanta, and still feeling the effects and the optimism of the 1996 Olympics, I (along with many others) was experiencing a bit of boom from the '90s that somehow seemed to go bust in 2001. The phenomena of the dot-com economy attracted quick money to businesses that started up fast, created an infrastructure that was only sustainable with the prospect of more venture funding, supporting the promise of going public or selling out, and riding the market to the top before it crashed. There were few who did in fact cash out, but many crashed. With economic volatility as well as a threat that we had never quite felt before in the United States, the dot-com days became known as the "dot-bomb."

I started my business in 1996, experienced a four-year honeymoon of success, and, along with several clients, went bust. More than a cash flow and credit crisis, I felt exposed and vulnerable as a young entrepreneur in his late twenties. The crash awakened a fear I had never experienced before and that impacted my perspective. It had its effects on my marriage, time spent with my young kids, and it influenced every decision I made, both personally and professionally. It was during this time that I was invited into a group of men who were CEOs running businesses under similar conditions and challenges as mine.

This team was led by a longtime mentor and friend of mine, Gayle Jackson. The team provided a shelter of oversight, authority, and counsel that helped me navigate through such a difficult season. It was in the context of this economic environment, where I was trying to discern and navigate the next steps in the midst of an inward anxiety that I had never felt before, that Gayle acted as a conversationalist. He facilitated a conversation that was truly life-defining in the area of stewardship. It has been over fifteen years since that conversation, and it is still as clear and crisp today as it was then.

Sitting in his office and using a simple pad of paper, he drew a line in the middle of it, with the assets on one side and liabilities on the other. Over the next hour he led me through a discussion, awakening what had been entrusted to my care, things that somehow my feelings of fear, fatigue, and defeat had eclipsed. What I felt seemed to govern the sense that all I had were liabilities. I couldn't see the true wealth of the resources, experiences, and relationships I had been given. Through such a grounding exercise, and through the discipline and practice of writing down a list of assets and liabilities that well exceeded anything monetarily, I saw my life with a whole new perspective, which created possibilities for the future I had not even begun to consider.

Stewardship of Abundance

Maybe you've been at this point in your life, or maybe you're here now, where you are so consumed with your liabilities that you have a discontented spirit that might be called a scarcity mentality rather than an abundance mentality, ultimately feeling like, "I don't have enough and I may never have enough." Such a mindset is suffocating. For you to engage as a conversationalist and act as a guide, leading people through what's been entrusted to your care, you have to go through this exercise for yourself: regardless of your net worth, difficulties, or the challenges you are facing in the moment, you have so much that has been entrusted to your care. As you pull your head up from the routines of daily life and look around at the landscape, you will find that regardless of the balance in your bank account, you have resources that have been entrusted to your care. And as you take time to steward these resources and manage them carefully, they will begin to care for you.

Fifteen years ago, the epiphany of that exercise was far greater than any business, strategy, or financial challenge I was facing. It left me in awe and overwhelmed because I had missed the meaningful gift of relationships. The greatest asset in my life extended to family and friendships, mentors and coaches, business partners and investors, and key client relationships. The sum of all of these were relationships that I still favor to this day, good connections that needed to be nurtured and maintained rather than neglected. These relationships were ones that were entrusted to my care, and they were a gift from God. My inward fear of circumstances and the threat of the day was potentially going to cause neglect in these areas, resulting in disobedience to care for my most precious assets.

I went from feeling discouraged that morning to being awakened with a renewed sense of purpose to invest my time and energy where it mattered the most. This discussion and exercise is one of the greatest joys I have experienced with so many since that time, acting as a conversationalist and facilitating the discovery process toward an awakening to what's been entrusted to someone's care.

Our work as conversationalists must start here—answering the questions for ourselves, which certainly is an exercise in creating gratitude that results in thanksgiving and that hopefully minimizes the fear in our heart, moving us to operate with a greater measure of faith.

The question of stewardship has to do with ownership. Who really owns the resources in our life? As Christians, we would hold that God is the owner, we are simply entrusted with the care of those resources, and we should care for them to the best of our God-given abilities. So the first step in this process of stewardship is recognizing who the owner is. Once that is answered, then we begin operating as a good manager. It is also important to recognize what has been entrusted to our care, and it's likely far more than we ever realized. Through a series of questions, we are able to draw out an awareness and give a sense of perspective that renews our thinking and stirs up a call to action.

As we consider a conversationalist's intention of how to spur one another on toward love and good deeds, to consider what's been entrusted to our care, these resources give the context for our lives when we have been awakened to what we have been entrusted with. That moves us to leverage these resources to love others and to see these resources put to good work.

Seven Stewardship Care Points

1. Revelation

The wisest man in the world once said, "Where there is no vision, the people perish" (Proverbs 29:18 KJV). Another translation reads, "Where there is no revelation, the people cast off restraint" (NIV). What is the vision for your life? Do you have a sense of where you hope to see yourself by the end of your days? Do you have a sense of where you hope to see yourself in the next decade, or even in the next few years?

When speaking about a vision, it is most common to think about a vision for a business or an organization, and then a person communicating that vision in a way that hopefully captures other people's hearts, inspiring them toward the vision so that they share a collective dream. As a conversationalist, however, you can begin drawing out the dream in a person's heart by the most significant and sacred of conversations. What is the vision that has been entrusted to their care? And more specifically, what has God revealed to them about their life?

People's response to such a question may vary to the degree of their connection with God or in the expression of their desires. For some it may be a specific act or accomplishment, while for others it may be defined as being faithful to the work that has been entrusted to their care. Some may have a clear picture of where they are heading, while others may have never explored the possibility of such an answer because their lives are bound by the day-to-day routine. Creating the space conversationally to explore and discover the answers allows you to be a witness to such a vision, and then to encourage and spur others on toward good works and love.

Such a discovery process is certainly inspiring. As you consider the impact of a vision fulfilled, what will be the result in other people's lives of seeing a good work accomplished, whether it be feeding the hungry, planting a church, starting a business, or taking up a hobby that becomes a full expression of that person's life? Once you enter into these kinds of discussions, whether the answers are being articulated for the first time or they have been thought through and communicated for years, there is still room to develop someone's thinking, clarity, and actions toward that dream becoming a reality.

Dreams and visions inspire people. Once they are communicated, they help spur people on toward their own vision and dream. For those who have experienced revelation, it creates a restraint, focusing one's life, commitments, and resources. More often than not, such a revelation is inspired by the Holy Spirit, but it is often given through the counsel of God's Word. His Word is the revelation, but when it is spoken in the context of your life, it is a promise that can be leaned into with the hope that in God's timing it will be fulfilled.

As a word of encouragement for those who have experienced a vision from the Lord: God is the only one who is able to fulfill it, and your work is simply to believe, be faithful, and align your life in that direction. Being invited into this level of trusted conversation gives room for many more conversations to take place, thus creating an awareness, an awakening, and maybe even an epiphany that compels them and spurs them on toward love and action, with the hope of seeing it become a reality.

2. Influence

We live in a day and age where we must consider the stewardship of our influence, particularly in the context of our social media and other forms of communication. Our words have weight, whether they are expressed through an e-mail, blog, Twitter, Facebook, Instagram, or any other networking site. We live in a day where many people are building their own platform for influence. But what are they influencing? Is it self-promoting and fame-seeking, or do they leverage such platforms for inspiring and spurring on for love and good works?

There is so much information available to us that it can be overwhelming at times, to the point where we can't even hear ourselves think. From a political standpoint, we have seen votes swayed and elections won because of the platforms of influence today. These platforms are not evil in and of themselves, but they are simply a means to be able to steward the message of our lives. More than ever before, this is worthy of significant consideration, inviting dialogue to the circles of influences and how we steward those influences, whether in direct personal connections or virtually around the world.

This exercise can begin at the coffee table with a napkin as you draw circles of influences around your life. The inner circles represent the more direct connections, while the most indirect are the outer circles. Drawing circles brings the appropriate level of overlap and intersection between groups and communities of people, giving a perspective whereby we draw out awareness of these circles, helping focus our energies and efforts to better influence. In a general sense, influence has to do with messaging—what is the message you are sending? What is the weight of the words you are using?

In the days of old, the exchange of letters over long distances carried weight that influenced people's thinking, encouraged them, and led them to a response that resulted in a mutual exchange. How we receive physical mail today is minimal—arguably nonexistent for some—compared to the virtual exchange through social media, video messaging, and even e-mail. What is the message of your life that you are communicating? Just like stewarding the vision of the dream of your life, so you are to steward the influence of your life and how people will remember you for the messages you have expressed and communicated.

The truth is that all of us have a message to communicate. When focused and stewarded, it has an unbelievable possibility to influence others for love and good deeds. More than ever before in history, one moment of inspiration captured in the form of a video can go from sharing one text to a viral movement that influences millions within a few days. I'm not suggesting we aspire to such public recognition, but that as conversationalists, we guide and draw out the message of our lives. This is an area of stewardship.

> All of us have a message to communicate. When focused and stewarded, it has an unbelievable possibility to influence others for love and good deeds.

3. Relationships

Walking through the exercise of writing down the circles of influence brings you closer to those people you have direct contact with. For most of us, this is family and close friendships. These are people we spend regular time with in close proximity; they may even be people in the cubicles at work or people we see regularly at our local coffee shop.

The truth is that most of us live in rhythms and patterns where we see people with whom we have some level of connection. These rhythms invite a moment of reflection to consider who these people are. We need to conversationally walk through the people who have been entrusted to our care, considering what we should do to be more intentional to nurture those relationships. This may be an occasional phone call, or it may include taking a risk in office conversations to move beyond news, weather, and sports. We should consider those relationships and the questions we could be asking to help draw them out. By taking just a few minutes of extra intentionality, we may unlock a whole new relational depth.

We are surrounded by people, and yet we miss some of the greatest riches relationally by not taking time to ask the simplest of questions. Again, one of the greatest ways to move friendship forward is to be a witness to people's lives in defining moments. There are defining moments happening all around us, yet we run the risk of being unaware or simply too busy to ask. There are no rules in this area relationally.

Whether it's by many or by few, we are taking the time to write down those circles and the names of people in those circles, reflecting for a few minutes to consider what is happening in their lives. You may be the one voice of encouragement during a difficult or defining season, when they are at the edge of having to make a hard decision. As a conversationalist, you may be able to facilitate an awareness that leads to an awakening for some of the most life-giving friendships with people living next door.

4. Resources

Resources may be the easiest of the seven talking points because it's the most measurable. However, it may be one of the most difficult points to access because most people hold their finances in confidentiality, certainly for good reason. Showing the details of your finances reflects one of the highest levels of trust in a relationship. Having considerable conversations around areas of spending reflects your priorities as well as habits, for good or bad. The percentage of your income that goes to savings, helping create a margin, reflects a discipline toward a threshold of margin in your life for unexpected expenses, for rainy days and difficult times. Where you invest your money for long-term or short-term gains gives an indication toward your risk tolerance, whether you're more conservative or aggressive. Looking at your charitable giving, and specifically where you give, reveals what you value most and what impact you hope to have based on your giving.

Talking about resources goes right to the heart. Where you spend your money reveals where your heart is at. As a conversationalist, you likely can only engage to the level of capacity for what you have experienced in those areas. For example, a seasoned CPA certainly will have a much different conversation than a struggling college student. Resource conservation has much to do with your experience, training, or knowledge in those areas. As a reminder, the conversationalist is not about giving advice as much he or she is about drawing out the values and the heart of the person stewarding those resources.

Rather than imposing your convictions, ideals, or standards, you invite them to consider what is important to them. Let them identify and define their own standards, establish their own convictions, and make their own commitment. Your role as a conversationalist may be biting your tongue and holding back your wisdom and experience until they discover and learn to steward for themselves what has been entrusted to their care. This a process of letting them mature into being a good manager of what has been entrusted to them. They may have a clear sense of what their threshold is of savings, giving, or investing, and we are only helping clarify their convictions. Then we can be a champion to see those aspirations become a reality.

The conversationalist can also draw out new ways of thinking about leveraging resources entrusted to them. From a business context, if you have a certain product, service, or technology, there may be creative ways to leverage those resources in order to engage in partnership agreements that help leverage the assets from other organizations to complement and expand your reach. The conversationalist may help give a fresh perspective on your available resources and ways to utilize them for a better return on investment.

One of the starting places for the conversationalist helping better steward what's been entrusted to another's care is by taking a fresh look at all of the resources that person has available, either in monetary terms, physical assets, or the people on his or her team. How would these resources be better stewarded? And if they are taking energy without a lot of return, invite the tough conversations about letting those resources go where they can be better put to use. Once again, when it comes to resources, you probably have far more than you realize entrusted to your care. A conversationalist will help guide creative ways to put those to work.

5. Work

What is the work that's been entrusted to your care? We need to make the most of our time while we are at work. In both theological and philosophical discussions, the subject of work often refers to a vocational calling that gives the expression of who you are. Your skills, your talents, and your abilities applied within an organization brings a contribution to its team members, its clients, and the overall mission of the organization. Within the context of this, you may have a job or a series of jobs that, during different seasons of your life, contribute to this overall work.

As a conversationalist, you can engage in full-time discussion, mentoring, and coaching, whereby you can be guided through how to bring your best use and potential within your workplace. There is no lack of opportunities, and the challenges that may follow them serve as details for engaging conversations. You are guiding toward a closer look to what has been entrusted into your care. What are the roles and responsibilities you have been given, and how could you better steward those so that they have a better impact for your effort and energies?

Certainly, you could talk at a level of task, performance, and even strategy, but often the most significant conversations regarding your work has to do with its purpose. What you do and how you do it is incredibly important. Understanding and operating from a place of why you do the work takes on a completely new significance, which impacts your intentionality when you go to work. So often people compartmentalize their life's calling—sacred versus secular—creating a distinction of who they are at work and who they are in their personal life.

Work provides a context for connections with people that may not happen otherwise. But your greatest opportunity to love people and impact them for good most likely happens with the people you spend your day with. Isn't it true that often the most difficult people are the ones who need to be cared for the most? Absolutely, it's uncomfortable; yet could it be that we are allowed for this time to come alongside of people who need to be cared for, so that some good can be done in their lives?

Talking with the people we have the opportunity to intersect with on a regular basis and exploring conversations with those we have the closest connections with often represents the greatest potential for breakthrough. Talk through how your performance at work intersects with people's lives. If you feel like you're in a dead-end job and it's lost its sense of purpose, challenge, or creativity, then it may be time to take a fresh look at why you are there. It is those conversations that add a spark to that office environment, influencing the culture of the team as well as the overall organization with a level of intentionality and engagement around stewarding the work that has been entrusted to you.

6. Personal Health

Your energy level impacts your effectiveness. You can be a great manager of what's entrusted to your care, but if you work hard at it to the point of burnout, creating stress in your life that ultimately leads you to having a host of chronic issues, what you've been entrusted with to steward will not be yours for much longer.

With all our technological advances and information on health and self-care, the amount of people dealing with obesity is in epic proportions. The amount of antidepressants that are being prescribed is in the millions each day. The amount of alcohol and substance abuse is at an all-time high. Even here in my home state of Colorado, we have legalized the use of marijuana for medicinal purposes. We are more stressed out and busy than ever before in history. People spend mass amounts of hours in front of digital devices, televisions, and computer screens, robbing them of the normal rhythm of physical activity that keeps the weight off and a healthy balance of mental activity and creativity.

You get to invite the discussion of what it looks like for you to be physically fit, emotionally healthy, and mentally sharp. Personal health and the definition of what that looks like is unique to every individual. But having such conversations invites new ideas and disciplines for ways to stay fresh, whereas old routines may not motivate in ways they once did. The conversations around these areas create their own accountability, either implicit or explicit, by raising the bar on our overall health and performance. It stimulates our energy.

People are living longer than they ever have before thanks to better foods and modern healthcare. But the question is, what is the quality of that life as it lengthens? Personal health at the end of the day really comes down to defining what disciplines you will do and then doing them, regardless of how you feel. In this case, your feelings will follow. We are only given one body, and it's for us to steward well. Without having conversations surrounding our health, we may just exist for the status quo until something happens that creates a situation that stimulates us to change. Engaging in conversations before such an event takes place raises the value on personal health and stimulates us toward love and good deeds, with our most precious asset being the body we have.

The apostle Paul speaks to Timothy, reminding him that physical training is of some value, but godliness is of value for all things (1 Timothy 4:8). The ultimate picture of personal health is spiritual vitality, a vitality that comes alongside personal care. As conversationalists, we have to consider this for ourselves. As we look around the circle of relationships, who is struggling physically or under the strain of emotional stress, maybe even crippled with the lack of mental clarity? Furthermore, what can you do to engage them toward great health?

7. Story

What's the story that has been entrusted to your care? Of all seven stewardship talking points, the subject of story is the capstone that brings together all these pieces. Yet within story there is a stewardship with how to communicate your story. What is it to be a storyteller? Through story a potential is created for connecting points to relationally engage people. You can help draw out other people's stories as you learn facets and details, inviting them into further dialogue to learn more. Story intersects with story and creates connecting points that take us further than if we just listed our preferences, opinions, or ideas about a given subject.

Our family just celebrated my son's eleventh birthday. Ten years ago, we brought him home from Samara, Russia, having adopted him. As my son, he is one of the greatest treasures in my life. With just these few comments about my son and our journey of adoption, a category is created that invites people into our story, which intersects with their story. It creates a category for who we are and that we have walked a road some people are only beginning.

If I told you that I started a business in 1996 that worked in every major city nationwide, and even in some international projects, it invites some discussion for fellow entrepreneurs and business owners and creates a category to spur on and encourage young entrepreneurial leaders. If I share with you that our family had over fifteen years of leading father/son and father/daughter retreats, helping facilitate moments these families would remember forever, it's a connecting point for us to engage in story. If I share that I transitioned from one career to a completely new industry, it invites a discussion. If I tell you that I have only been a part of two churches ever since I was fifteen years old, it invites a variety of discussions from navigating changes in leadership, managing disappointments, to maybe even being committed to a community of people regardless of the circumstances.

Likewise, if I tell you this week is my anniversary and my sweetheart and I are celebrating twenty-two years together, having been married in a little country church in north Georgia in 1994, our marriage story may spur you on in your own marriage. I may tell you that at seven years old, I sat in an old swing with my grandma at her country home where I prayed to receive Christ, and then later, as a fourteen-year-old up in Montana at my aunt and uncle's camp, I dedicated my life as a teenager and a commitment to the Lord Jesus Christ—that also invites someone in to share in my story.

By listening to these few stories, you get a picture of who I am by the experiences that I have had and the testimony of my life. And for every story I share, it's like an invitation for you to invite me into your story. It's the intersection of stories that creates the potential for spurring one another on to love and good deeds.

Lost and Found

Just like my story in the events of 2001, I had lost a sense of what had been entrusted to my care. As a conversationalist, you can engage with these seven talking points, which will help stir and stimulate your thinking to what's in your care, how to best steward these things, and, as you do, will help you engage with others. There is no limit to where you can conversationally go, and there is no limit to the potential for life change and impact as a result of stewarding your life to be a blessing to others.

INSIGHTS AND ACTIONS

1. Do you have a scarcity or abundance mentality? Explain.

2. What are your assets and liabilities? What resources or assets have been the most underutilized in your life?

3. Evaluate these areas of stewardship:

   a. What *vision* has been entrusted to you?

   b. Where has God given you *influence*? How are you stewarding your circles of influence? What are the messages that you are sending?

   c. What *relationships* do you need to be more intentional with?

   d. Where do you want to invest your *resources* to make the greatest impact?

   e. What is the *work* that has been entrusted to your care?

   f. What can you do to better care for your *personal health*?

   g. What is the *story* God has written for your life that needs to be shared with others?

4. Since we are not owners but *managers* of what God has given to us, which two of the seven areas of stewardship listed above do you want to focus on in the coming months? Discuss this with your conversationalist partner this week.

5. Who will you ask about his or her stewardship this week? Which question below would be most appropriate for your relationship with this person?

   • What vision or work has been entrusted to your care?

   • What are you doing to steward your circles of influence?

   • What does it look like for you to be physically fit, emotionally healthy, and mentally sharp?

   • Other: _____

Chapter 12

SECRETS:
WHAT THOUGHTS HAVE YOU NEVER SHARED?

Recently, I spent some time with Kyle, a dear friend of mine. We've known each other for about eight years, and we've experienced a lot together. He is in the process of moving his family back to the United States after a two-year international work assignment. Their time away has knit their marriage together, given them time with their children, and strengthened this man who borders on the miraculous compared to when I first met him.

Ten years before, a vulnerable time in his life and a few casual exchanges at work led him down a path of compromise, resulting in a long-term affair with a coworker. As he would recount his story later, it was a period of isolation, which is ironic because as a Christian man going to church and working for a nonprofit organization he may have described himself as being surrounded by people but feeling totally alone. He was cheating his companionship between living a lie with his wife and a fantasy that was fueled by lust for an attractive young lady at work, which left him feeling trapped, scared, and completely empty. It was a crisis of compromise: "How have I fallen so far? Who is this man I have become? I don't even recognize the man in the mirror anymore."

In a moment of raw vulnerability and conviction, he did one of the most courageous things a man in his position could ever do: he confessed to his wife. He broke off the relationship with the young lady, removing any contact from his phone or e-mails. And after a courageous act of getting clean, his wife asked him to leave. He is a successful executive today running an international division of a company; in fact, you would have no idea that ten years ago he was homeless living out of his car. And what marks that season so well is that when he needed a friend the most, he had no one to call for help.

"Get right, make it right, and get on the right path." No one wakes up in the morning seeking to destroy their life. No one has a vendetta to hurt themselves or those around them. Yet for all the good that is in our life, we still have to navigate the choices that would tempt us beyond our ideals and principles. For my friend Kyle, a little flirting led to a forest fire of disaster that took years to mend. What causes us to veer from the path of the straight and narrow? If we can learn from Kyle's story, it may simply be that a life of secrecy led him further into isolation, removing him from good, healthy, and encouraging relationships. It was these very relationships that would spur him on toward love and good works, as well as protect him during times when he was too weak to make the right decision for himself.

There's no one who is free from temptation; there is no one beyond making foolish (or even evil) choices. Jesus Christ has given us what we don't deserve in his mercy, he's given us what we could never earn in his grace, and he has chosen to love us no matter our failings. We are only a whisper away from a confession and receiving his forgiveness. When you consider the secrets of your life and the thoughts you've never shared, consider the possible impact of that on your own life.

Paul writes to Timothy, instructing him and giving him an invitation to the possibility of a life that is clean and has no secrets. He writes that "the goal of this command is love, which comes from a pure heart and a good conscience and a sincere faith" (1 Timothy 1:5). Imagine with me for a moment what your life would look like if you lived with a heart full of love; imagine your life if you lived these attributes to a greater measure. What's the potential of those you could impact by being an extension of God's love, grace, mercy, and forgiveness in the relationships in your life? What is the one thing that may be limiting you from a life of this kind of fullness?

As conversationalists, we must answer this question for ourselves first before extending it to others. I'm certainly not imposing the idea that we should shout our secrets to the world. Rather, we are only identifying those people we hold in the utmost trust, exercising our authenticity and vulnerability in areas of our heart and our thought lives, for the purpose of being truly liberated.

You may be reading this knowing that you have been carrying a burden of secrecy for months that has limited you from receiving the fullness of God's love. It may be time to release that. By doing so, it opens you up to greater capacities to be able to consider other people's lives and how to spur them on toward love and good deeds. Yet because of your secrecy—whatever level, measure, or degree you hold back—you may find yourself surrounded by people feeling like you are wearing a mask or a sign around your heart that says Do Not Disturb.

When you bring the light of conversation on these areas in your life, it opens you up to be loved in the places you need most.

This may be the most important place for you personally, in which you need freedom from the burdens and secrets you have been carrying for far too long. I began this book by sharing why people tell me their secrets, thereby suggesting that you may have a few people in your life whom you believe are truly safe, people who believe in you and who can help you. As you move into those conversations with a trusted few, they will help guide you toward healing and defining next steps. This is a process, not an event, and yet it begins with bringing your secrets into the light.

Conversations are like life-giving oxygen, reviving places in your life that may have felt suffocated. When you bring the light of conversation on these areas in your life, it opens you up to be loved in the places you need most. It's a living example of the gospel of grace, the good news that we hope to receive, and as a result we can then extend that same grace to others. This truly is the work of the conversationalist, that as you grow in grace, you to extend it to others.

Blessings and Curses

As we engage as conversationalists, let's consider the root behind the secrets and thoughts we never share. When you look at a life of compromise, to whatever degree of deception or darkness, it is is living a lie. And we know that in order to live a lie, we have to believe a lie. Somewhere deep within our psyche, we began believing messages that may sound common, such as these: "I am not good enough. I am too much. I am not enough. I am not pretty enough. I am not strong enough. I am not smart enough. No one cares. I am alone." Such lies may be followed up by beliefs that say, "I will never be . . . " These are lies that, at some vulnerable point in our lives, were spoken over us, and whatever evil was present at that moment we received and believed, and it influences our hearts and minds today. The results of such thinking lead us to take action that reflects the evil of the lies we have believed.

Deep within the psyche and human design, every person longs for and needs some level of affirmation, approval, and a strong sense of identity of who they are. Lies are the very messages that work against those needs in ways that result in something that is artificial, superficial, or even corrupted. If lies are the threat, then the antidote is truth: What are the truths we believe? And it is these truths that dispel the power of such evil in our lives.

One of the greatest ways you can grow in your ability to receive and extend such grace is to understand truth and have a shrewd discernment of lies, being able to identify and bring those into the conversation, allowing the truth to bear on whatever lies have held the heart captive. In the most practical way, you can enforce truth by speaking blessings in return. To bless is to extend affirmation, approval, and identity through words of truth. As people begin to receive those words, believe them, and operate from a place of such truth, it liberates their lives. As you are listening to the stories that give context to the secrets someone has carried, you can identify the curse of a lie spoken, received, and believed and boldly declare, "That's a lie!"

It's critically important to help navigate the conversations around secrets and thoughts that have never been shared before with the assumption that, once the secrets are shared and they have been brought to the light of the day, they are able to set that person free. Your role as a conversationalist is to understand the environments these people are in, which affirms and echoes these lies, thus helping them take steps to get out of an environment that would continue to cripple them. The work of a therapy group, small group, dinner group, and even a team within the workplace that is grounded in speaking truth and blessing—operating from a place of high trust, authenticity, and vulnerability—is creating an environment of confidentiality that truly sets people free in ways that seem miraculous.

Stumbling Blocks

As a conversationalist, you can help guide the conversations to evaluate areas along this path and the turning points along the way that help identify the stumbling blocks that represent a pattern that consistently trips people up and makes them fall. So far, we have looked at passion, strength, attitude, and stewardship, which are four areas where secrets come into play. What are the stumbling blocks that trip you up, keeping you from operating out of a full heart and the expression of your passion? What compromises your strength? What steals the joy and robs you from the attitude you hope to consistently display? And what stumbling blocks keep you from stewarding the resources entrusted to your care?

There may be twelve or twenty that you can come up with, but it is important to narrow your focus to just two or three you can clearly define. If you looked at the pattern of Kyle's work, his travels, and his overall drive, it would not take long for the casual observer to notice that he was seeking approval, finding his significance and identify from his work. In the process of trying to be a good provider, his pace and performance ultimately robbed him from intimacy with his wife. It created a distance within their marriage and closed off their hearts to their deep love for one another. When his work took a turn, and no matter what he did his need for significance was not met through his performance, then his need for affirmation and approval was found in the arms of another woman. This good man was in the wrong place at the wrong time, and the stumbling blocks that caused him to fall may have been removed if he had a trusted few friends, with whom he could invite some tender conversations on thoughts he had never shared before.

Strongholds

As you consider the secrets of your life and the thoughts you've never shared, and as you engage in these dialogues with others, one of the greatest areas of bondage and burdens that keep people from true liberty and healing is unforgiveness. Regardless of the offense and the pain, whether it is emotional, physical, or financial, long-term withholding of this grace from another is actually withholding this grace from you. The prolonged effects of unforgiveness festers and becomes infected, resulting in something malignant with a long-term loss to the vitality of your life.

In the most tender and graceful way, you need to identify the people in the other person's life to whom they need to extend grace, mercy, and forgiveness. Such a stronghold results in feeling like a victim to some unjustified offense, and so they carry themselves in a victim mentality, operating in a mind-set that the world owes them. In some form, this reflects a selfish mentality, which creates a stronghold that limits their ability to truly serve another person. One of the greatest ways we can serve another is by listening to their story and navigating conversation through it, thus inviting them to a place of asking, "Do you ever think you would find it in your heart to forgive this person?"

As people forgive others, it releases them from a curse and invites a blessing of freedom and grace into their lives. It releases hate, malice, or anger, potentially unlocking compassion where there was once criticism and condemnation. Exploring and discovering such a stronghold, you may find that the person they need to forgive is themselves. Such an act invites a peace into their lives, opening up places in their heart where they can receive love for the first time.

As you navigate such a sacred dialogue with someone, celebrate with them, for such an act releases them to be who they truly are. Such liberty extends a grace to so many other people in their life—family members and friends—and it releases health and wholeness into every area of their life. In the midst of pain, forgiveness unlocks a joy of secrets revealed.

> In the midst of pain, forgiveness unlocks a joy of secrets revealed.

Private Thoughts

If you are in this place of quiet and deep confidence as a conversationalist, realize there is no pattern or program to any of these conversations. The truth is that it is raw and vulnerable, and frankly, it can be uncomfortable at times. But as you stay steady through these conversations, you may notice some themes surface as other talking points that, once shared, may help you engage. Not all secrets and thoughts are ones of compromise and loss; more often than not it's a mixture of both pain and potential. These themes I have observed are in five areas: success, fears, failures, regrets, and desire. As a conversationalist, you may find yourself navigating the tension within all of these themes within one setting.

Success

I enjoy seeing my friends succeed. Just recently I sat with a CEO who had finished a grueling board meeting after several years of difficult transition. He proposed some bold initiatives that were so full of courage that even his staff thought he was a little crazy; yet such a courageous act was well received by his board, compared to just trying to survive the last few years. This leader rallied the board to a unanimous vote to implement those key initiatives, approving the budget and making the necessary investments into those initiatives. He was glowing. This organization's reach is around the world, and so this decision represents an impact on thousands of people, and the heart of this man, staying steady and persevering through difficulty, was in a place of success and victory. As a conversationalist, I got to walk through the details of such a transaction and all the events leading up to that decision.

Fears

The second theme has to do with fears. There is no doubt my friend has fears that are fueled by doubt disunity among the team may have ultimately impacted a vote. Such fears may cripple and keep people from moving forward to courageous actions, and after all the calculations, they may find themselves in analysis paralysis. Their minds are filled with a hundred different scenarios that might go wrong. At some point, however, a boldness is required and fear, if not addressed, may keep people from moving forward. The conversationalist often has the gift of hearing such fear and speaking love and truth over it. At the end of the day, though fear was present, it did not win. You can engage in present discussions, but it helps bring in past perspectives of other successes and other fears that, either crippling or overcome, allowed you to move forward.

Failure

Like with the discussion of stumbling blocks, so often what keeps people from moving forward and the thoughts they hold close is the threat of failing once again. The fear of failing one more time makes us feel like a fool. No one wants to be a fool. So, often we resolve never to put ourselves in a position again to act foolishly. Thus, we run the danger of never taking a risk. The goal of not being the fool may be the very reason they are stuck. As a conversationalist, in the right timing and openness, you can help them by guiding them through discussions around past failures. This may feel exhausting, yet within such failures are little nuggets of learning, wisdom, and grace that can be brought into the present, giving you strength and courage for the decision ahead.

Regrets

What if my CEO friend had held back when he knew he needed to push forward? Knowing the timeliness of the decision and what was at stake, what if he took a more conservative route? Would he be talking in terms of his regret? What if his leadership style was more marked by things he wished he could have done but didn't do? What if the compound effect of regret minimized his influence and respect and his ability to make decisions?

The subject of regret is on the softer side of our secrets. Identifying these patterns and the language around them (usually expressed in statements like, "I wish I could have if . . . ") is important. You can turn the conversation around: "*When* you have the next opportunity, what will you do?" Regret for some may fall under the category of resolutions or establishing patterns of making goals and never seeing success. Broken resolutions and unmet goals over a lifetime create a negativity that diminishes healthy ambition and aspiration. It may leave you feeling withdrawn or apathetic, even stepping into something that may lead itself to success in your life. Wherever you find yourself conversationally navigating the themes of successes, fears, failures, or regrets, the combined work of these discussions lend themselves to desire.

Desire

What stirs your heart? This is a simple question, yet the answer may create an inner turmoil that feels impossible to answer. You can help draw out desire, moving someone from an answer of "I don't know" to an expression with clarity. Desire is more than just preference; it is the expression of the longings of your heart. Desire may be initially expressed in broad categories, like material possessions, positions of recognition, and the power to influence, and any one of these can be corrupted. Desire takes time to fully be expressed, and it most often reveals the most noble aspirations.

Words like love, faith, hope, impact, and legacy describe what matters most to us. These concepts run so deep that they are rarely discussed, and yet they represent what is most important about us. It's not necessarily right or wrong, yet it's completely unique to every single individual. When desire is expressed, it gives focus, purpose, and drive. When it aligns with the Word of God and the conviction of your call, it's a reason for living from a full heart. You are going to wake up and be fully alive. When someone gets clarity in his or her desires, it won't be long until he or she begins moving in that direction.

Secret Responses

When you are engaged in this space, then you are soul-deep in sacred discussions that are reserved for the precious few. It is truly an honor to be here. If you treat it in any cavalier manner, you may find yourself never invited back into this level of interaction again. As you are stepping into this space of listening, perhaps for the very first time, your response is less engagement and more empathy to receive and extend with grace. For someone who has never shared a secret of their life, it's not something that has even been rehearsed before, so they may not have a lot of practice—so how it comes out may be messy. Stay steady and receive them in grace; they are coming to you because you represent stability in a vulnerable place. They are taking a big risk in talking to you.

Your first response should be an acknowledgement of gratitude: "Thank you so much for entrusting your story to me. I just want to say that I love you and value you," and then affirm them, reminding them that their story is safe and confidential. Such a reassurance goes a long way in helping settle in the place of vulnerability. If during the discussion you find yourself at a place beyond your comfort level, or at the limits of your knowledge or training, then know the extent of your role in their story.

One of the greatest ways you can serve as a conversationalist is by guiding the conversation so that through the discovery process, if there's a certain volatility in their life that is threatening, you can recognize they need outside help. Your role may be listening to the story to the point where you can understand, and then your part is that of a connector, connecting them with someone who can help walk through this time of difficulty or challenge. It may also represent an opportunity that has to be seized in a particular period of time, in which your skill set and experience is limited to the help that you can provide. If at any point you discover an area of their life that represents neglect, abuse, or something that is life-threatening, then you must make it clear that you need outside help.

Another grounding point for the conversationalist walking through discussion with someone who may have shared about their life for the very first time is that your response goes beyond the moment. More often than not, there's the thought or response of regret. After the conversation, they are wrestling with the thought of, "I should have never shared that." This is your opportunity to engage with courtesy and care. Within a few hours or the next day, follow up with affirmation and gratitude. Whether commenting on further reflections for you or questions for them, you are ultimately acknowledging that you are honored they would share with you. Once again, a recommitment that their story is safe and confidential does a lot here. Part of your role as a conversationalist is to bring stability into one of the most vulnerable places in their life, and so these few comments right after a point of sharing does much to begin strengthening the place that feels weak.

As a final note, and maybe one of the greatest importance: no matter the level of secrecy in someone's life or thoughts, whenever you find them at a point where they are ready to come clean, it is your opportunity to express love and remind them of how much God loves them, even in their brokenness. God's love for them is so unwavering that, despite their actions, they are still worthy to receive grace and forgiveness. It is the kindness of God that leads us to repentance (Romans 2:4).

Repentance is the idea that simply says, "I am going to turn from my way of thinking or acting to a direction that is honorable instead of dishonorable, that's wise instead of foolish, and that's one of embracing truth and believing it over entertaining lies." Repentance is living a life not bound by curses, but having them broken so that you can truly receive a blessing, which can be an overflow of your life to others. In this way, the secrets and the thoughts that you've never shared may be one of the greatest extensions of grace from your life to another.

INSIGHTS AND ACTIONS

1. How have burdens of secrecy weighed you down?
2. What would your life look like if you lived life "from a pure heart and a good conscience, and a sincere faith" (1 Timothy 1:5)?
3. What secret thoughts steal your joy and are limiting you from this kind of fullness?
4. What areas of possible unforgiveness could be holding you back from the fullness God intends for your life?

5. What success in your life have you been hesitant to share because it seemed prideful or misunderstood? Let someone celebrate with you.

6. How can you be mindful of your responses when someone shares a secret with you?

7. What is the root behind your need to keep a secret? Why do you feel you cannot share that secret with another person? What truth will bring you freedom?

8. Since secrets cause many to stumble and confession is good for the soul, which of the five thoughts would be healthy for you to bring into the light: success, fears, failure, regret, or desires? Discuss this with your conversationalist partner this week.

9. Who will you ask about his or her secret thoughts this week? Which question below would be most appropriate for your relationship with this person?

   • What's one thing I don't know about you?
   • Who can you share everything with in your life?
   • What would it look like if you lived a secretless life?
   • What secret steals your joy?
   • Other: _____

Chapter 13

GIFTS:
WHOM CAN YOU BLESS TODAY?

My wife and I attended an event that was one of the most heartfelt and moving experiences we have been to in a long time. Our church and community sponsors Dream Centers of Colorado Springs, with one such expression being Mary's Home. The dream of Mary's Home, which has now become a reality, is that it would be an apartment complex designed for single moms who were once homeless. These were moms who were living on the streets of Colorado Springs, trying to survive each day, just keeping their kids fed and in school, doing whatever they could for income.

What we witnessed that day was a graduation ceremony. These single moms had once lived on the streets, but now they were dressed in cap and gown, with their nicest outfits on. Having done the hard work of classes and training that would help set them up for success in raising their children, finding work, and building friendships and a strong community around their family, these women were graduating. They had also experienced healing from the traumas they have experienced in the past, which helped strengthen them, developing a competency and a character that will allow them to stand on their own two feet one day, taking them from a place of surviving to thriving.

They walked onto that stage to receive their diplomas, shaking hands and taking pictures, receiving a beautiful bouquet of flowers, and they walked off the stage into the arms of their children, who were waiting for them. I witnessed a turning point in each of those families. They are now a part of a community that will help them succeed and love them deeply along the way. There were a lot of tears of joy that day, including mine. It was such a beautiful and memorable moment that started with a dream of caring for those in our city who were the most vulnerable, led by the vision of my pastor, along with other leaders in the community who rallied to see such a work established.

Mary's Home was more than just one person's dream; it was the dream of many that brought it about. It had a far greater impact when generosity went beyond the individual, when the collective focus was aligned with a strategy toward really making a difference in someone's life. The subject of gifts and whom you can bless is far more than just a few dollars given away sporadically. Rather, it has everything to do with a heart of generosity. Before it can make a difference in your world or in your city, it is something that has to start with you. Whom can you bless today?

There was a CEO who runs an organization of about two hundred employees. Beyond the company's normal charitable year-end giving, they started something new during Christmastime. They gave everyone on their team $100 in order to bless another person or organization they were passionate about. There was no limits or rules attached to their $100; it was simply to be given away to those in need. As you can imagine, the culture of that organization was spurred on toward spontaneity, creativity, and generosity within each its employees. The impact resulted in hundreds of stories being told around the office in the days to come, during staff meeting, lunches, and in water-cooler conversations, creating joy. It was a gift not only for the people who received the money but it was a gift to the people who gave the money away too.

Proverbs 11:25 says, "A generous person will prosper; whoever refreshes others will be refreshed." Generosity within the heart of an individual invokes a prosperity that's to be measured in far more than just resources back into his or her account. It's not a prosperity gospel I'm talking about here; rather, it is about having a generous heart. As you seek to refresh others, then, in turn, you will find yourself refreshed.

Take a few minutes to consider the opportunities you have had to be generous, where you were able to give in such a way that others were refreshed when you saw a need. Think about the names of those people, look at their faces, and remember the experiences around giving. What did it feel like? In the end, were you refreshed? Did your generosity bring a joy into your life too?

One of the Greatest Adventures

Each of us can take the little we have and give it away, and that little could mean the world to someone else who is in need. What has been given to you in order to bless another? As a conversationalist, this one question hits the pay dirt of practicality. It's where you align your passion, strength, attitude, resources, and even your secret thoughts in order to be generous. Recognizing the gifts you have received and whom can you bless today puts these ideas into practice. This is the result of considering how we may spur one another on toward love and good deeds.

> Each of us can take the little we have and give it away, and that little could mean the world to someone else who is in need.

The encouragement and exhortation of such a question takes time for your personal reflection, causing a spurring on to take place. Giving becomes sacrificial, and when done with an open heart of generosity it invokes blessing. The idea of love and good deeds is that it must first connect with the heart. To give reflects an open heart—the most significant gifts are the ones connected to love. The way you love the people you give to is connected in the most practical way of your act of generosity that results in good works.

Just like with Mary's Home, these ladies and their children are one day going to stand on their own two feet. They will be contributors in friendship, church, community, and in the workplace. They will have a strength that may not be present today, but they will likely find ways of identifying other ladies and young families in vulnerable places, and they will do their part to see them strengthened and encouraged.

Generosity begets generosity. When you catch the heart of it, it takes on a life of its own, bringing significance, meaning, and purpose into everything you do. As a conversationalist, you get the opportunity to engage conversationally with the simple questions of: What gifts do I have and whom will I bless today?

Blessed to Be a Blessing

Imagine if you were sitting down with somebody you knew was part of the organization that had been given $100 to give away, and you learned that person was struggling with what to do with that money. How would you guide her in her discovery process? How would you help him be intentional with how to give that money in a way that would maximize the impact of such a gift?

You wouldn't want to presume your knowledge about their gift, so you might ask them what they have to give away. Such a beginning to a conversation gives the context for the resources they have available to them. Then out of mere curiosity, you may ask, "Why do you want to give?" or, "Why is it important to give?" Any "why" question will typically reveal the heart of the giver. Once you find out the question of why, then you may want to narrow your focus more and ask, "Where do you want to give?"

After you find out where they want to give, then you may want to explore, "Whom do you want to give your gift to?" which could be to an individual, a group of people, or to an organization. As a final question that brings clarity, you could ask, "What do you hope the impact will be as a result of your gift?" Such questions may be too formal for an informal relationship, yet you can contextualize the questions or soften them up. What you are trying to do is a lead the person through a disciplined discovery process of seeking clarity, which helps reveal what is most important to them, what they value most, and so help them direct their gift accordingly.

Imagine now as a conversationalist that, after going through such a discovery process, you learned that this organization who supplied a one-time gift of $100 was so moved by the heart of generosity and the stories of impact that they then were going to give their employees $100 to give away every day. Suddenly, the fun of the conversation takes on a tone of seriousness, feeling the responsibility that this organization has entrusted to their care. The questions previously asked are even more necessary in order to explore and discover how to best honor the giver and bless the receiver.

Such a story seems almost fantastic and possibly too good to be true. Who does such a thing? The idea of a company giving $100 away at Christmas, let alone $100 a day, in order bless other people adds perspective. Your personal economy may be that you make $100 an hour versus $100 a day or even $100 a week. We have friends who are serving as missionaries to people in Honduras who make $100 a month. The amounts are actually secondary to a heart response of giving. For those of you reading this who actually make $100 an hour, then giving $100 a day can represent a tithe, allocating roughly 10 percent of your income.

Depending on how we look at it, this triggers a heart response that is sacrificial. Let's put it in perspective of giving away $100 a day to the person who makes $100 a month. What could be the impact? It could be a funding project to help create a social enterprise that would actually put seeds in the ground for a future crop or animals that could reproduce themselves. This could one day move a villager toward a lifestyle of sustainability with good stewardship. The conversationalist draws out of the heart the possibilities and potential impact of generosity. Even the discussion cultivates a cheerful heart of giving that blesses another.

Gifts of Blessing

What are the gifts that you've been given to bless others? If you are in the place of having a $100 a day to give away, then you may put your best effort to faithfully distributing those resources to all the people and places imaginable. As you move forward into that space of giving and seeing people's different responses, you may find different themes of the impact of those funds, as well as your sense of joy and satisfaction with certain people or organizations more than others. With a flow of resources from a generous heart, you will quickly find that you give to what you care most about, in addition to where you see the greatest impact from your fruit and generosity. As you continue to give, you may find that there is something presented that is a larger need than your $100 a day, requiring an accumulation of multiple days so that you can be more strategic with your larger gifts.

The greater vision for the impact of those resources, the more strategy is required to be a better steward. If stewardship is wealth management, then giving is wealth distribution. There is no formula or right or wrong answer, other than it comes down to the heart of generosity. Jesus referred to the widow's mite as the greatest gift given because she gave all she had, whereas the rich young ruler was asked to give away everything and follow Jesus, but the sacrifice was too great for him. Money and the resources we give are a reflection of our heart. As we are working through conversations and we hit a wall, the person who acknowledges their desire to give yet gives nothing may be ready for a gentle consideration or reconsideration of what they already have.

I witnessed a sweet moment at a stoplight some time ago. A young mom, with her children in tow, was driving an old minivan that was missing the hubcaps. She pulled up next to a man holding a sign and gave him a bag of unopened chips. She didn't give him money; she gave away her groceries. If there are clothes in your closet that haven't been worn for a year, or nonperishable goods in your pantry that haven't been touched for months, you can take them down to the local mission and find that there is a line of twenty or thirty people who may benefit from those items.

When it comes to resources, once you have made up your mind to give, the rest is actually a lot easier. Physical resources often have a measurable impact from your generosity. The heart of the conversationalist moves you beyond the "have-tos" of giving to the "get-tos." It's training and equipping people with the mind-set that asks, "Whom can I bless today?" You can look around the people in your life and the experiences you've had and see what resonates for you. Then you can move forward in a way that intentionally engages your sweet spot for giving.

Giving moves us toward action, making a commitment toward what we believe in and value the most. As a conversationalist, you are discerning those care points in an individual's life that may represent a soft spot for them because of their story. Then, with counsel, you can help guide them through the best way to utilize their resources that goes beyond just giving away finances. This includes your time if you are limited in resources.

My friend Dave has organized work days for companies in Denver, where the company would donate time and their people to go serve someone in the community. Now many of the organizations Dave has served have gone from one work day a year to giving one work day a quarter. Such a generous spirit within a company is contagious because of the stories of impact along the way. Again, generosity is only limited by your creativity. As you engage in it, it awakens a desire to live your life in such a way where you can give of your resources and time to bring a blessing to others.

What Happens When People Give?

Generosity opens the heart to believe. The apostle Paul explains that our generosity results in thanksgiving to God (2 Corinthians 9). More than food, clothes, or any direct benefit from a gift, generosity does something that no argument, persuasion, or opinion may ever do. It opens people's hearts for gratitude toward God.

And as we engage in the adventure of a generous life and we are faithful to that adventure, God promises to provide the supply we need to be generous if we steward those resources well.

As we faithfully give in the ways that align with our passions and our purpose, and as we give to those who are in need, we cannot begin to comprehend the impact it will have on the hearts of those people. Watching the joy of an entire community of those who have contributed, as well as the recipients of Mary's Home, resulted in thanks and gratitude to God. As people open up their hearts to the things of the Lord, and give praise and thanks to him, it gives them access to his presence, where they can experience his love and grace.

Through our relationship with God, we catch the heart of the one who is most generous, who sacrificed his son, Jesus, on our behalf. We catch the heart of the Father who is most generous, and the one who wants to give his children good gifts. As conversationalists, one of the greatest ways we can invoke a heart of generosity is by catching the heart of the Father. What's on God's heart, and where is he giving? As you model that for others, there is a generosity that's caught, not taught. You lead by an example, seeing a need and helping to meet that need, then inviting other people along and giving them the opportunity to invest. It's in this place of mutual generosity where we come alongside one another and contribute whatever time, money, or resources that we can. We are contributing collectively to a community that can receive it; thus, it is a blessing to others.

The work of the conversationalist is about inviting dialogue that always moves us to a heart level—within these conversations, something moves us to close the gap from where we are today and where we hope to be in the future. When we can close that gap in the most practical way of the commitment of our time and our resources, it's truly life-changing. What we are truly describing with this generous spirit is really the heart of family, the heart of friendship, and the heart of authentic community. In a word, it's the church, and it's this church that should be the most attractive place on the planet for people to come and be blessed.

Spiritual Gifts

If you have received Jesus Christ as your Savior and Lord, then the Holy Spirit indwells you. Your body is the temple of God; you are a carrier of the presence of God. No matter how you feel or think, this is what is true about you because God has said it is so. As you align your heart and mind more to his Spirit, and as you yield to his leadership in your life, you will find the expression of his personality taking place through you, revealing the characteristics of God through your life. As you walk closer in an abiding grace, you will see these characteristics more alive than ever before, affecting your attitudes and actions.

The Holy Spirit also expresses himself through gifts. These gifts are on deposit in your life, and they represent the anointing of the Lord, which is waiting for the appointed time to be released. This is not so much for your benefit only, but for the benefit and blessing of others. It is these gifts that are available to you and are only a prayer away. Yet if you read the Scriptures carefully in regard to these gifts, then you often see that they are actually called out by brothers and sisters in Christ, who may see a gift inside of you but that is not yet active. Paul said to Timothy, "Fan into flame the gift of God, which is in you through the laying on of my hands. For the Spirit God gave us does not make us timid, but gives us power, love and self-discipline" (2 Timothy 1:6–7).

It's these same leaders who will come alongside to speak a blessing and pray over you. It is these gifts that are waiting to be released, not just in a Sunday morning service but on every day of the week, through the expression of your life as you interact with people. The gifts of God are his tools for building up, comforting, strengthening, and encouraging one another. As we look at how to spur on one another toward love and good deeds, it's accessing more than just secular or conventional ideas about a person's life.

Rather, it's about having a spiritual discernment to be able to consider what God has placed as a deposit inside of them. It is about having spiritual conversations, and once these gifts are called out, they are released and fanned into flame, which has an impact on loving others and expressing that love through good works.

One of the most impactful things you can do as a conversationalist is explore and discover the spiritual gifts of those you are connected with. Learn about them, pray over them, and dream about ways to put them to work in order to be a blessing to others. In regard to the gifts that you have been given and the blessing that you have to give to others, I encourage you with the words of Paul in his letter to the Romans: "I long to see you so that I may impart to you some spiritual gift to make you strong—that is, that you and I may be mutually encouraged by each other's faith" (Romans 1:11–12).

> Conversations are waiting to happen that will allow you to give of the gift within you, which is expressed by your time and resources.

Who are the people you long to see? Conversations are waiting to happen that will allow you to give of the gift within you, which is expressed by your time and resources. As you exercise these gifts in the most gracious ways, they may result in true life change. We have been given far more than we could ever imagine. In fact, all of us are the ones who have been given that $100 to give away each and every day.

As you consider what has been given to you, you can find ways to bless others from a place of abundance. As you are on this journey, I pray that you would have eyes to see the people in your life, to discern their gifts and resources that have been given and entrusted to their care, so that you can call them out and encourage them to use those resources as an investment in the lives of others. It is my hope that you would encourage them to sow seeds of gratitude and future generosity that would help even the weakest and most vulnerable become strong and full of grace. You are blessed to be a blessing. It's time to conversationally unlock the heart of generosity.

INSIGHTS AND ACTIONS

1. What blessing have you received from someone else that has made a significant difference in your life? Describe the impact.

2. What gifts do you have that you can use to bless others?

3. If you were given $100 to give away today, what would you do with it? What if you were given $100 a day to give away—how would you be more strategic in your giving? Where would you give it?

4. What has it felt like to give generously (of all yours resources, not just money)?

5. Do you know what your spiritual gifts are? What are the top three? How are you using your spiritual gifts to bless others?

6. When was the last time you dreamed about new ways to use your spiritual gifts? Write down some fresh ideas today.

7. Since generosity opens the heart to thanksgiving to God, what one gift do you feel God is highlighting in this season for you to share with others? What is one area that you want to give to more in the future? Discuss this with your conversationalist partner this week.

8. Who will you ask about his or her gifts this week? Which question below would be most appropriate for your relationship with this person?

   - If I gave you $100 right now to give away, to whom would you give it?

   - What gifts do you have that comfort, strengthen, and encourage others?

   - Who in your life would benefit from a word of encouragement from you today?

   - Other: _____

Chapter 14

LEGACY:
HOW WILL YOU BE REMEMBERED?

You're catching me on the one of the most significant days on the year. As I'm writing this, it is Cari's and my twenty-second wedding anniversary. It was this day when my sweetheart walked down the aisle, and I couldn't take my eyes off of her. She was fully aware of all the details surrounding such a day, whereas the only detail I really cared about was her. What a joy it is to be able to celebrate the fact that most of my life has been spent with my best friend. She truly is the love of my life.

If you and I were spending some time together in my office, you would quickly discover the most important things about my life are my faith, my family, and my friendships. You would notice the pictures of people who mean the most to me all around my bookcases. The biggest pictures in my office are of my wife and me, sitting among the Georgia foliage, taken on a fall afternoon in 1993 when we were engaged to be married. You would see pictures of my children, whose smiles warm my heart every day. You would also see some older pictures that are either faded or black and white. Within these sets of pictures, there are six faces that all represent a generation. Six generations of my forefathers, all unique to themselves but consistent in being faithful to God and to their family. It's these pictures that represent my heritage. When I take the time to read through some of their stories, it intersects with my story and does something that strengthens me from the inside out.

No family is perfect, and that includes ours—we have a colorful past. But through my papa's line, there are seven generations of faith. This type of heritage seems to be rare and almost nonexistent in a culture trying to rid itself of godly values and redefine the family. The reason these generations are so important to me is because I come from a broken home, and the events and circumstances around my life ultimately led to my mom and dad making a decision to separate, which defined my life. I love and honor both of my parents, yet the healed hurt of such a decision has put a powerful call on my life, to be faithful and steady regardless of the difficulties I face.

Every one of us faces difficulties. The question of character is, what will we do in the face of that difficulty? So often it's during these times that we feel like we are standing alone, but as we look around, as the book of Hebrews describes it, we are surrounded by a great cloud of witnesses (Hebrews 12:1). They are cheering us on and encouraging us by the testimony of their lives. It's hard to imagine the people who are praying for us, and the impact of their prayers, and so it is with us as we engage in praying for others. This is what fortifies us spiritually and allows us to persevere in these times, as well as taking moments of beautiful celebration and responding in gratitude and thanksgiving. The picture of your heritage, however strong or broken, helps define the legacy you hope to leave. How will you be remembered?

> The picture of your heritage, however strong or broken, helps define the legacy you hope to leave. How will you be remembered?

If we were to walk out of my office onto the front porch, you would find two rocking chairs. Though it seems so old-fashioned in a modern age, you would find me there on most summer mornings about the time of sunrise. These rocking chairs remind me of my childhood days at my grandparents' farmhouse; they also represent thousands of hours spent in early morning devotions, watching some of the most extraordinary sunrises of my life. They represent memories of conversations with good friends over the years, either over a morning breakfast or an afternoon sweet tea. It's the environment of this setting that causes one to slow down—looking over the wildflowers of our front pastures, seeing our dogs run around and our horse grazing, waving at neighbors as they walk by. It creates space for one's mind and soul to reflect on what matters most.

Let's imagine I was toward the end of my days, and instead of forty-two I was ninety-two. It is this setting that lends itself to the depth and sincerity of the questions: "How will you be remembered? What are the things about your life that mark you by a deep joy, satisfaction, and fulfillment?" As you sit there rocking, feeling the cool of the breeze, it allows you to settle in and it helps me to share in the story of your life. By listening, we conversationalists will be able to identify different themes and points of excitement as a highlight in others' journey, and embedded in these stories are what they value most and where they invested their life.

Prosperity for Posterity

When Cari and I were first married, we had a mentor couple who invited us into their home and their lives. You could measure success in so many ways in the lives of Russ and Julie Crosson, yet to me their greatest success was in what they did in raising their family. Russ would often talk about the difference between investing in your prosperity versus your posterity—there is, in fact, a difference. There are far too many stories of those whose ambitions were for their family's prosperity at the expense of their posterity. In the search for success, they lost what was most significant in their life.

Those early discussions raised the value for a man in his early twenties to the type of family I wanted to have. A few conversations with a man I respected and who modeled the ideals I hoped to emulate had a deep impact on my rocking-chair reflections, even in my twenties. Since that time, I have traveled all over the country, interacting with successful executives and business owners who, once you peel back the layers of their story, have a quiet tragedy of the cost of building a business. Pursuing what the world would see as successful and prosperous has come at a great expense to their marriages, families, and even friendships.

Of the seven life-changing questions, if giving is the pay dirt of practicality and the sum of the previous five questions, then legacy is the expression of character, habits, and the perseverance to be faithful toward loving and good works, representing the sum of your life. Again, no one is perfect and without fault, and no one is free from difficulty and the hard times that would tempt us all toward compromise, leaving us in a place of regret and shame. The question of legacy and how you'll be remembered flies in the face of those difficult times. What will you do during those times when you fall? Will you humble yourself, turn, and do the right thing, restoring relationships where they've been broken? Will you be faithful to the good work that God has placed in your heart?

Breaking Chains

As you are thinking about your life, you may find yourself over-whelmed. I have shared many conversations with people who feel like they don't have such a heritage. They don't have models from their past who represent the kind of life they hope to live and the legacy they hope to leave. At some point, all of us fall into this category of having to manage the disappointments of those whom we once held in esteem and who may have fallen from grace. As you consider this, and as you guide people conversationally into the legacy they hope to leave, there must be a discussion of what chains must be broken. You have the opportunity, no matter your background or your past, to break the chains that have bound your life. You do not have to be bound to the fate of your forefathers or the poor models you've witnessed—their voices don't have to define you.

Far beyond your family lineage, genealogy, or even the pictures from your own past, as a Christian you have a heritage that claims you as a son or daughter. You have a heritage that, despite your brokenness, you have been adopted into the family of God. You have been claimed. Where there may have been a sense of feeling orphaned or abandoned, that is no longer the case—you belong to a family where you can cry out to a Father who loves you. You are part of a community of sons and daughters who are now your brothers and sisters in Christ, fathers and mothers, and grandparents in the faith. This is your spiritual heritage that is based on the blood of Christ.

You have been redeemed, and so you are clean and free from any bondage of past mistakes. You are forgiven. There are those with the same grace who would welcome you into this family and care for you and celebrate who you are, which gives you a sense of security and well-being in your soul. This causes you to dream about the legacy you hope to leave one day, and you declare like Joshua did in the days of old, "But as for me and my household, we will serve the Lord" (Joshua 24:15).

Breaking the chains of the past leads you to declare the kind of family you will become. Like a creed, this is what we are known for, the character that we will exhibit. And from that character proceeds our reputation, and over time we will become known as a family who is faithful, a family that is known for the ideals that we hope to live out. As you declare such a future, it moves from your heart to your mind, a statement of faith with boldness and conviction, even if it is lived in a quiet way. This runs so deep within your marriage that it gives your children and grandchildren a sense of security, belonging, and safety in the midst of such volatility in our day. This is something worth fighting for.

And of any conversation, this is why we need one another. We must engage conversationally to consider how we may spur one another on toward love and good deeds for the legacy that we hope leave behind. This may be the hardest thing for us to do, which is why the spurring on and the good works are required to engage, despite the difficulty and even the occasional feeling of overwhelm.

The conversationalist will help encourage and move you forward in leaving this type of legacy. As you consider your own life and circumstances, I want to encourage you, especially those of you who are parents and grandparents with prodigal sons and daughters who have turned away from their faith. First of all, it is hard, and there are no easy answers. Trying to honor and love those who seem to have fallen for a counterfeit love is a grief indeed. But I pray that God would bring people along your path to encourage you and build you up during this time of difficulty. Don't lose hope.

A good friend of mine called me recently about his teenage son. We have been praying for this young man for quite some time, since he had been growing more and more distant. At eighteen years of age, he was acting out in ways that were really an embarrassment to himself and his family. My friend modeled a belief in an action, rallying those he trusted to pray and intercede on behalf of his son. The combination of the events of a dad's sickness that weakened him helped lower the guard of his son, combined with the discovery of some inappropriate photos on social media, led to a tough discussion that ultimately led to the question between a father and a son, "What's hurting in your heart that you are trying to fill it up?"

This led to a beautiful discussion of an eighteen-year-old son who, despite pride, arrogance, and rebellion shared of his loneliness, hurt, and anger, which led to a place of forgiveness, turning the heart of a son toward a father. What a beautiful story that, after a few months of what felt like a tragedy, turned into a blessing. And now father and son will be meeting with a counselor together, and they will walk through some of those hurts and together find some healing. My friend would say the miracle he experienced was a result of a company of people praying for his son's heart to turn back to the Lord.

If you are personally experiencing this type of situation, or if you are working with somebody through that time of difficulty, one of the greatest acts you can do is rally the saints to pray for the turning of hearts. So often people acting out in ways unbecoming of who they are reveals an area of their life that is hurting and needs healing. It's these precious moments brought on by pain that truly represent the breaking of chains. Instead of responding to rebellion in anger and embarrassment, you embrace a life of grace and forgiveness, extending the same love of God that has been extended to you.

For those of us who have received much grace, we have the opportunity to extend the same to others, especially those we love the most.

For those of us who have received much grace, we have the opportunity to extend the same to others, especially those we love the most.

If you walked through such a difficult season, and we were to find ourselves back on the rocking chairs of my front porch, our conversation may have moved from such painful moments to the joy of redemption. Then we could discuss what would be different moving forward. What priorities would have shifted in your faith, your family, your friendships, and in your finances? You and I might explore the conversation that may redefine the kind of man or woman you hope to become and how you hope to be remembered by those you care about most, resulting in new or renewed priorities. When you discover or rediscover these priorities and declare them, even in a quiet conversation in a rocking chair on a front porch, it creates an accountability for yourself and others. Once you take action, it gives room for ongoing encouragement and celebration when you see the fruit and the blessing of making investments into what and who will become your legacy.

Why this day is special is that it marks over two decades of life with my sweetheart. But I am also reminded of a conversation that once took place between my father-in-law and his daughter. He once asked Cari, "Who is the man you want to marry? What is the criteria of who will be your husband one day?" Motivated by a simple question, she wrote down a list of the qualities of the man she hoped to marry. Followed by further conversations with her dad and mom, that list became a point of prayer as well as a protection for when she had guys who wanted to date her.

By some miracle, a young man who was far from perfect signed up at the last minute for a mission trip to the Appalachian Mountains, and providence would have it that we got assigned to the same work crew. While swinging hammers, hanging sheetrock, and serving those in need, conversations started that, over months, turned to friendship, and six months later turned to a romantic relationship. Even today, considering who I was then, I was the least likely guy to ever become this precious lady's husband. Purely by the grace of God, I met the full criteria on the list that she once created. It's a beautiful story of how two young sweethearts become companions for life, and yet it is a story of the conversations that lend themselves to the kind of legacy we hope to have.

What if my father-in-law never took the time to ask his daughter about the kind of man she wanted to marry? What if Cari had not taken the time to pray, think, and search the Scriptures for the kind character she hoped to see in her husband? I would later learn that my father-in-law's parents, my wife's grandparents, had been praying for her husband since before she was even born. It's hard for me to even write about this when I think about the calloused arthritic knees of a grandmother sitting bedside in Omaha, praying for God's protection and grace over a young Georgia boy. God heard and answered the prayers of my in-laws.

Until the Next Generation

Since my youth, God, you have taught me,
    and to this day I declare your marvelous deeds.
Even when I am old and gray,
    do not forsake me, my God,
till I declare your power to the next generation,
    your mighty acts to all who are to come.
(Psalm 71:17–18)

If you walk into my in-laws' home today and stand in their foyer, you will see a treasured case that holds within it stacks of Bibles that represent my wife's heritage. These Bibles, tattered and worn, represent six generations of my mother-in-law's and my father-in-law's families, representing missionaries, pastors, and business leaders whose lives have been marked by faith and faithfulness to pray for those who would represent their legacy. I am not only the beneficiary of my family's prayers but of the prayers of my in-laws as well. We were given a pattern, in which Cari and I have been praying for our sons-in-law and daughters-in-law since before our children were born. To think about our spiritual legacy, who can even imagine what the results of praying for two decades for our children and our children's children? Maybe only in heaven will we fully understand the result of such prayers.

The work of the conversationalist certainly is one who guides and directs, drawing out the heart by asking questions, by listening, and by engaging. But the conversationalist is the one who considers the heart of these people by spending the time praying and seeking the Lord on their behalf, even before the conversation begins. As you catch the heart of the Father on behalf of those you are engaging, as you spend time in his presence interceding on behalf of those you love, he will give you insight, wisdom, and understanding on their behalf. And what a confidence we can have as we seek the counsel of God on behalf of those we love.

When we get a sense of what is on God's heart, we discern the questions that help us navigate the hearts of the people we love, drawing out the depths of who they are and helping them become all that God has called and made them to be. In time we see this impact the decisions of those they will date, the spouses they will marry, how they will raise their children, the kind of friends they hope to keep, and how they conduct themselves in the workplace.

The question of legacy and how you hope to be remembered aligns your life and allows you to live in a way that is consistent with your faith and values. Such a discussion goes far beyond rules, and it is instead motivated by relationship, so that that your life becomes a blessing. Such a question may be the most life-changing question you have ever asked: How do you want to be remembered?

INSIGHTS AND ACTIONS

1. How would you describe the legacy that you have been given?
2. What things do you want to discontinue and what things do you want to carry on?
3. Who have been your spiritual mothers and fathers in the faith? What specifically about their legacy do you want to carry on?
4. How do you want to be remembered?
5. What do you value most that you hope will be remembered and carried on for generations?
6. If you have children or grandchildren, what kind of conversations do you need to have about their future? How can you turn their hearts toward God and his plan for their life?
7. Who can you ask to pray for you on behalf of your future, legacy, and children? Who do you want to be praying for more consistently?
8. Name five people over fifty years old who you feel are running their race well and will leave a legacy that you respect.
9. Since your prosperity is for your posterity, how do you want to realign your priorities today for how you want to be remembered? Discuss this with your conversationalist partner this week.
10. Who will you ask about his or her legacy this week? Which question below would be most appropriate for your relationship with this person?
    - How do you want to be remembered?
    - What in your life do you hope will stand the test of time?
    - What needs to shift in your faith, friendships, family, or finances to align with the legacy you hope to leave?
    - Other: _____

The Disciplines of the Conversationalist

You can have a heart with the capacity for meaningful conversation and the questions to gain access, but key disciplines move us from good ideas to building life-defining relationships one conversation at a time.

Chapter 15

ENGAGING
THE SEVEN DISCIPLINES

The work of the conversationalist includes having the right heart. Rarely have I found a person simply walks into conversations which engage in the seven life-changing questions, let alone one of them. There must be some heart preparation that first takes place, and it is this preparation that conversationally sets the environment and readies the person for the potential of a life-changing discovery.

As you grow as a conversationalist and your relational equity with people builds, it allows the potential for you to move forward into these conversations in a way that seems amazing. You may be separated for months or even years, but somehow the distance and time don't seem to matter when you re-engage. When you connect, you connect deeply, in a rich and meaningful way. These are friendships that are nothing less than a gift from God. And as your life builds conversationally, the fruit of friendship will build alongside it, leaving you feeling wealthy beyond anything you can financially measure.

We are building the wealth of relationships, which are marked by defining life moments. As you become a witness to these moments, having the privilege of being able to walk alongside during times of transition, challenge, or even opportunity, it makes the celebration that much sweeter. In addition, you may find that when you're at a point of need, you'll have people who walk alongside you in the same manner. Yet for all the heartfelt preparation, if such a discovery process is left to our own isolation in disengagement, we may be robbed of the full blessings of relationship and community God has intended for our life.

Engaging the Disciplines

I've been a longtime practitioner and beneficiary of spiritual disciplines. As I have taught on this subject over the years, I most often refer to Jesus's teaching to his disciples in John 14:21: "Whoever has my commands and keeps them is the one who loves me. The one who loves me will be loved by my Father, and I too will love them and show myself to them." It's this beautiful language of the promise of his presence that actually gives us the hope of God, which reveals his heart to us as we operate from a place of knowing and obeying his Word while keeping the right spirit by loving him and others.

I've illustrated this using a simple Venn diagram of knowing, being, and doing. Depending on your season of life and where you are at in your spiritual journey, the circles of this diagram move and have different points of emphasis. Your personality and the sincerity of your passion might even come into play here. When I was in seminary, I felt like the circle of my knowing was at the largest point of my life, doing was at the second, and my being felt the smallest and, in a general sense, it felt somewhat artificial. Yet other times in my life have been a high-service season where I'm not learning much, but I am spending most of my time engaged in acts of service. You might say it's an emphasis of doing. If this is prolonged, it may lead to a time of burnout, and it is time to change.

When we reset our emphasis on to who we are, our being, heart, soul, and spirit need to be renewed and recalibrated. These are wonderful tensions that give expression to our spiritual life, which apply to the conversationalist as well. If the heart of a conversationalist is being, and the questions of the conversationalist are knowing, then the disciplines of the conversationalist are the doing. In wonderful tension of the three, as we integrate God's Word into the conversations of our life, the beautiful mystery is that God reveals himself to us. This moves us to the first of the seven disciplines.

Discipline #1: Confidence: Removing the Barriers of Engagement

If we are to relationally engage, then we must be aware of the anxiety that keeps us from engaging in the first place. On some level, every conversation represents a risk. When we engage in relationship, every question has the potential to reveal the heart of everyone involved. When somebody feels exposed, they may react in ways that are not so loving.

So often in relationships our insecurities flare up insecurities in others. I don't pretend to understand why this happens, but I see it in myself, among the friends of my teenage girls, and within groups of high-level leaders. Our insecurities may be the thing that keeps us from engaging relationally, thus limiting our ability to be conversationalists. When you think about the word *confidence*, it sounds more like a characteristic than a discipline. To operate in the place of confidence, however, is a discipline that you have to take action on. The action is removing the barrier that keeps you from engaging with others.

Confidence is different from pride, ego, or arrogance. I am man enough to say that I was actually watching a series with my wife from Beth Moore called *Audacious*. Audacity is not the absence of fear; rather, it's in the midst of our insecurities that we have to muster the confidence and courage to engage in the presence of our fears.

What is the source of our confidence? It can be mustered and expressed because of our personality, our skill set, our training, or even our experience. Even in the midst of all of these, moving to the next level and asking the question represents a certain sense of vulnerability, having the potential of flaring up an insecurity or a lack of confidence. We've talked about this in the area of passion: if you are still working through some pain that needs to be healed, asking somebody else about their passion may in some way reveal an area of pain in your own life that needs resolution. This is the beauty of the conversationalist—we haven't fully arrived, nor has our confidence reached its full maturity, yet we are healing as we are helping others heal.

What is the true source of our confidence? If you know God's ways and obey them, and if you operate in a place of love and grace, then God promises to show up to you, revealing his heart and his presence. It is because the blood of Christ has been sprinkled on us that we have experienced forgiveness and grace, which then allows us to have confidence to enter into a deeper relationship with God. As we spend time with him, and as we approach him with confidence, we receive a confidence that goes beyond any sort of natural ability or understanding. When we experience the love of God, it fills us with confidence that our lives are not subject to any normal threat. Even in the midst of a threat, we press forward because we know that nothing can threaten us from God's love. This builds up strength and confidence inside of us, which allows us to face uncertainty.

Having been filled with the grace and love of God, we approach relationships with the same grace, extending the same love we have received. This gives us boldness to ask questions in a way where we have once experienced timidity. In the spirit of the conversationalist, if you have people in your life whom you want to engage further with but lack the courage and the confidence to do so, the more time you spend in God's presence, even praying for those people, the more he will give you wisdom, insight, and understanding in your conversations with them.

The writer of Hebrews says that without faith it is impossible to please God (Hebrews 11:6). If you consider that every conversation represents a potential risk, then you'll grow in spiritual maturity. *Faith* and *risk* are actually synonymous terms. Small faith will result in a small tolerance of risk, and a great faith will be one that trusts God in a way that extends your ability to engage in risk. Certainly, this needs to be kept in balance with wisdom, yet any faith, once exercised, honors God and delights him. If you engage relationally with others, especially if there is a sense of risk involved, it may threaten the comfort of the relationship, but exercising such a faith actually honors God. And when you honor him, he will honor you.

By engaging in confidence as a discipline, it actually strengthens you and builds up your faith (like a muscle, which, when exercised, is strengthened). You will find that it multiplies itself conversationally, resulting in enriched relationships.

Discipline #2: Circles: Defining the Who (People, Places, and Priorities)

When you are looking for a home, more often than not the real estate agent who is helping may guide you through a process of defining the circles of where you live your life. You begin looking at your commute to work or school, where you shop for groceries, the gym where you exercise, the church you attend, and friends who represent your community. Not only that, but you also look at the circles you would like to be in. This type of discussion helps narrow your search to where you want your home to be. If your home is too far away from those places you frequent, then your attendance at those places may diminish over time.

In a similar way, defining the circles of influence in our own lives is actually a natural exercise as we look at the rhythms of our life. Yet we often don't take the time to do this until we have a reason to do so. Like a real estate agent with someone looking for a new home, the conversationalist will guide you through defining the circles of relationships in your life. These may represent only a few relationships, or they may expand to different geographical regions depending on where you live or work, and depending on different experiences and memories made with those people. These are friendships with people you see on a regular basis, which can be defined by people, places, and priorities.

People

When you look at the subject of people, start with your calendar to see whom you have interacted with in the last week, month, or year. Going through your calendar, looking at meetings that were scheduled, phone calls that were made, even people you have Skyped with over long distance is really helpful here. The discipline of defining and drawing circles begins with making a list of all the people in your life. I'm not talking about cutting and pasting your LinkedIn or Facebook lists; this is actually taking the time to write down people you have physically spent time with over the past year. This begins the process of thinking how to be more intentional with those people.

Places

Define the circles further by writing down the places you visit on a daily or weekly basis, or even those places you visit occasionally. Going back through the calendar again is helpful here, helping you to think through meetings you've had, conferences you've attended, places you've traveled, and events where you have served.

This will remind you of people you met and interacted with more spontaneously, yet the spontaneity may have sparked a significant conversation.

Just a couple weeks ago, I was sitting in New York City with a friend of mine. It was one of those engaging conversations where we were reflecting on our history and some of the defining events over the last five years of our relationship. We also talked about an inflection point he is now facing. So I had the opportunity to engage the discipline of considering him in the circles of my life, engaging in the opportunity to be an encouragement in this season of decision. The intentionality to schedule something once or twice a month over the next ninety days is a discipline that will bear much fruit in the future.

The discipline of defining circles of places also includes where you are going. Since moving to Colorado in 2002, Jeff represents one of my oldest Colorado friends who now serves as a missionary in Honduras. We spent over an hour on the phone this week catching up. We also talked about our plans for this summer, because my daughters are going on a trip to Honduras with their youth group. I am still thinking and dreaming about the possibilities going down to Honduras as well, or maybe I need to give my girls the space they need. A few scheduled conversations with my friend, regardless of whether I go on the trip, will help me guide, prepare, and pray for my girls as they get ready to go on their trip.

Priorities

The discipline of defining the "who" serves as a brainstorming exercise that begins to surface priorities of where you need to be spending your time and how to engage them conversationally. Whether you spend five minutes or a few hours going through this exercise, it will help you narrow your focus on your commitments. You may learn through this discovery process that there are priorities that may be secondary, and so it's time to put some boundaries on some of those priorities so you can engage in others. Awareness to your commitments and realigning your priorities requires hard work, and yet there is a great reward when you do so.

Circles of Influence Meet Significance

Drawing the circles of influence now connects with the circles of significance, giving you perspective of where people fit from casual to catalytic circles. It's this discipline of writing down names within the circles that helps evaluate and create a plan to intentionally engage in your relationships. For the student, it may be family and friends, church and school. But as you grow, mature, and take on additional responsibilities, your circles grow.

We all have circles of influence. Taking the time to write down the categories of influence in our life and then writing down the names of people within those circles, even if some of the names overlap, actually helps to build our prayer and life journals. Even the process of writing down those names, visualizing their faces, their families, their businesses, and their stories that come to mind, makes it much easier to pray for them. Even starting with sending a simple text, saying, "I'm thankful for your friendship," can do a lot to build a relationship.

The act of defining your circles and writing down those names may leave room in your heart and mind for creative ways where God can prompt you to reach out as an encouragement to those people. For some of my social friends, even the permission of this idea would light them up to connect with hundreds of people. However, for other friends, this discipline may result in taking action in an intentional and deep way to one person each week. That way, over the course of a year, they would have fifty meaningful connections, building the relational groundwork for life-changing conversations.

Once these circles are defined and written down, it gives you the opportunity to go back and review, write down little details, and add people to your list. Even for me, usually on a Saturday or Sunday, I will take time to write down the names of every person I had a conversation with that week. Every time I do this, I am caught by surprise that my heart is filled with gratitude for the relationship, and I am often overwhelmed with the privilege to be able to engage with such meaningful areas of their lives. The work of the conversationalist and the disciplines that follow are about intentionally engaging with those people toward life-changing conversations. This discipline will give you the road map to be more intentional in your relationship.

Discipline #3: Connect: Clarifying the Expectations

A strong connection comes with healthy expectations, which sets the environment for a great engagement. You must prepare your heart so that you're fully present to whatever degree of flexibility or formality is required. Even though we may be clear with what's in our heart for the time, we must also express and communicate those expectations to the people we meet. Clarifying expectations is a discipline that will move us along conversationally.

Toward the end of my seminary studies, I worked on an independent study with the focus of mentoring and closing the generational gap within churches. We conducted a survey that extended its reach to about eight hundred people, with over two hundred giving a written response on the subject. One of the questions was whether or not a person prefers a formal or informal setting for mentoring relationships. The response was almost split down the middle: nearly half the people preferred a formal process to one that was more spontaneous and felt like they were just hanging out, and vice versa. During the same survey, nearly 65 percent of the people who responded experienced disappointment in their relationship, either as a mentor or the one being mentored.

The discipline of clarifying expectations is critically important to be able to help minimize disappointment in any relationship. The survey gave evidence that those who once reached out to either mentor or to be mentored, if their experience was negative, were more likely to never engage in another mentoring relationship. Within this discipline of clarifying expectations, we must first pause and look at our needs, then evaluate what needs we are trying to get met through this person. If the person does not deliver on our expectations and need for fulfillment, will that lead to a broken relationship? There is a lot of psychology to consider in this question, yet it begins as an expectation of being served versus serving.

The truth is that we all have needs, so we must understand the source of how those needs are going to be met. Placing these burdens on relationships may be too great for the long-term health of particular relationships, so the discipline of connection must start with a healthy discernment of our own needs as well as the needs of the people we are meeting with.

There are some people who really need a formal environment to feel safe and let their guard down. It sounds counterintuitive, but some are more on guard if they don't know what to expect of their time with you. Yet for others, setting a formal agenda may feel like you are suffocating the spontaneity and diminishing the pure enjoyment of the meeting. As we grow in our ability to connect, it serves us well to understand the people we are meeting with. Some people want to meet so they feel like they are accomplishing something, having a defined result, as well as some action steps for the next engagement. Others may find that the highest value for our time together is simply to be heard and the gift of having a safe place to share a story, a struggle, or even a success, which is the greatest gift of friendship.

As a general principle, the greater the significance of the event, the greater the need for clarifying expectations.

> The greater the significance of the event, the greater the need for clarifying expectations.

After spending many hours in private conversations with CEOs, I have observed the quarterly tension points of meeting with the board. Board members do not like surprises; they want to have all the information in front of them so that they can discern a clear pathway for the organization and its leader. The amount of time and preparation for such meetings is significant not only for the leader but for the staff as well.

A great board meeting is one where the agenda is presented in advance. The details of that agenda, such as supporting documents, are presented before the meeting even begins. Then a presentation by its leader during the meeting clarifies the issues at hand, thus laying a foundation for healthy discussion. The board members who do not honor the preparation and commitment to engage or deliberate over the issues at hand may find themselves off the board.

Setting expectations by a principle of understanding the significance of an event must be discerned for the conversationalist. An event for you may not be as significant as for the person you are meeting with, but understanding the significance of an event, whether it's with a formal agenda or just hanging out, ultimately honors the people you are spending time with.

Answering the question of how to best honor the person you are spending time with is a discipline of clarifying expectations. What can you do to prepare for that time together, which will hopefully move your relationship forward? Clarifying expectations applies to every circle of our relationships. In practicality, it doesn't have to be overly burdensome or complicated. It is as practical as sending a text the morning of a lunch, letting the other person know you are looking forward to your time together, confirming the meeting place and time. By doing this you are clarifying the expectation of the time together. This goes a long way to creating a strong connect so that when you meet you can take time to consider the most important questions you should be asking.

Discipline #4: Considerable: Asking Great Questions

We were recently up in Breckenridge with four couples, skiing and enjoying the Colorado winter. After nearly six inches of fresh powder and some great times on the slopes, we relaxed later that afternoon, watching some football and spending a few minutes in the hot tub so our muscles could relax. We had an incredible dinner prepared, which set the environment for great conversations around the table. I noticed Susan quietly making her way around and asking some of the ladies, "What are you looking forward to the most in this next year?" I didn't hear all of the responses, but I certainly saw her discipline and graceful way of asking a wonderful question.

Considerable questions are not just about asking the right questions, but also about asking them in the right manner, in a way that is received with sincerity and an open invitation to engage. What Susan modeled was a quiet discipline that invited each person into relationship and opened the door to some possible stories that will prompt the conversation to go deeper. It's these invitation questions that allow you to identify some of the details of what's important to the person, which can't necessarily happen in a group setting. Whether the exchange is only two minutes or twenty minutes, it may finish with a further invitation to continue the discussion at another time.

Invitation questions invite you further into relationship so you can have a clear sense of whether it is well received. Invitation questions also have a key role for the conversationalist, because answers may not be fully developed and ready to be shared. "What are you looking forward to in the next year?" is such a simple question, and yet when somebody of great sincerity and respect asks it, you want to take time to answer.

The person you are asking may be completely consumed with trying to manage their day-to-day responsibilities, and the thought of actually pulling their head up and looking around to respond with equal sincerity is difficult to do, because they haven't yet had the opportunity to think through the answers. Invitation questions, however, allow the people who have thought through the answers to have an opportunity to express them. It invites the one asking further into the details of the answer. This could lead to more questions or an opportunity to speak into such a desire.

There are invitational questions that you refer to on a regular basis, and, depending on the level of relational engagement, they move you to the potential of a considerable question. If an invitational question is framed indirectly and in a nonthreatening way, then a considerable question could be asked in a more personal and specific manner that is direct to your life and what you care most about. If the limit of your invitation question extends to, "What's up? What's going on? How's it going?" then you may have room to develop your questions so they are asked with a greater level of sincerity and uniqueness.

When Susan asked, "What are you looking forward to most in this next year?" it was asked in a way that one got the sense that she had already answered the question for herself. Having some history with Susan, I know from experience over years that this is a big question for her personally. Out of mere curiosity, a sincere answer on your part would give you a window into her world and some of the things that she's taken the time to prayerfully think about may spur you on and encourage you to greater things in your year. This is the great exchange, moving one to potentially considerable questions.

> Considerable questions are ones that move us closer to the heart of what's going on in a person's life.

Considerable questions are ones that move us closer to the heart of what's going on in a person's life. These are questions that are asked in a personal and maybe even a private way, inviting you to go below the surface and get to answers that have never been shared before. It's with considerable questions that you may get responses like, "I've never been asked that before."

The discipline of asking questions is about being ready with questions to ask. My hope is that at some point while reading this book, something would trigger in the stories, ideas, and the questions presented, spurring you on to have considerable conversations with others. We are raising the bar with how we interact with the people in our life. Think for a moment of what you could ask a person you're meeting with, that they may have never been asked before. Write down a series of questions that may be more invitational, indirect, and open. As you think about that list of questions, upon further reflection, prayer, and maybe even a little rewriting of such questions, what questions will you actually ask them?

The heart of the conversationalist is not to play games or challenge for the sake of challenging; this isn't about who has the guts to ask the hardest question, though there are times that is needed. No, the heart of the conversationalist is about taking time to consider the most important questions we need to be asking.

What if you did this exercise with one person, and then connecting it with the discipline of defining circles, you begin to write out and define the questions you should be asking with other people in your life? As you go through this exercise, you may find that there are some theme questions that seem to deeply resonate for you, and so defining and refining these questions will help train you to become a better conversationalist. By doing this, you will have the questions in your mind so they are ready when the environment is right.

You certainly can lean in further in the seven life-changing questions; however, you may find that you to have warm up the conversation (and thus the relationship) until you can get to the heart level issues before you can ask a life-changing question. In this discipline of asking the question, it is critically important to remember that every question must be matched with sincerity.

Before you move to the next discipline, include in your list your most common questions. What are the questions you ask on a regular basis? Think about your interactions, meetings, and events in the last week. What were the questions you have asked, and what were the questions you didn't ask? What are the questions you would like to ask but have never clarified or had the courage to ask? As you write down such a list, you may remember questions you wish you didn't ask, questions that took you to places you really didn't want to go or belong in, either because of confidentiality or gossip. It is important to become aware of these questions.

The last list in this discipline is questions you wish others would ask you. What were the meetings with people you care about where, because of a lack of time, distraction, or simply because they were unaware, you wish they asked that one question? On the surface, this seems somewhat self-seeking, yet identifying these questions reveals a care in your life. If you take the time to ask others what they care most about, that is the foundation for a considerable question. Listening to what they care about most allows you to respond with further questions of a more considerable nature. It moves you and the conversation closer to the heart of the person and what's most important in their life.

Discipline #5: Coaching: Let's Get Moving

There are people in your life who, after you spend time with them, motivate you to be more and to do more than you were before you met with them. After spending time with these people, your world feels a little larger and you feel more encouraged and equipped to live with a brighter hope and a sense of fulfillment. It's the spirit of that connection and that gift of friendship that, as a discipline of a conversationalist, is a coach.

These kind of relationships are very rare, yet they do exist. These people have a way of being able to see into your life, drawing out the right questions with the deepest level of care and sincerity, leading you through a discovery process where you are able to understand your faith, values, and highest priorities, even tapping into your greatest passions. And whether it's explicit or you feel it from the inside out, they spur you on and move you in that direction.

In 2011, we were facing some difficult challenges because of some changes in my business. It was during this time that my heart was open, while seeking what the Lord's will was for my life, that I knew we were facing an upcoming transition. When I was experiencing a time of disillusionment and discouragement, truly feeling lost with what to do next, Ephesians 4:1 hit me in the heart: "I urge you to live a life worthy of the calling you have received."

Something in this statement was a challenge, a charge, and a sense of urgency all at the same time. Before I felt like I had been put on the sidelines, but now it was time to step back into the game. It was time to exercise my faith into the unknown, diminishing whatever fear had crippled me, knowing that God had made me for more. I had no clue what was ahead, but I knew there was a call on my life to serve God. Even though I was fully secure in my salvation and my sonship in God's family, I was living in a way that seemed unworthy of the measure of the calling I had received. I knew I had a part to play in God's plan, and it was time to get up, take a stand, and start moving forward.

During this time, our family was given one of the greatest gifts in friendship by being introduced to Fabi and Kathrin, German nationals living in Berlin and serving as pastors, who our church was supporting. We had the opportunity to host them in our home during a time where they had a front-row seat to the story of our lives. It was a defining point in my life, and God gave me the gift of friendship in the most unlikely way.

I learned that Fabi was also at an equally vulnerable place in his life. Such a crucible of our lives was the furnace for our friendship. Fabi began asking questions, speaking into my life, and walking with me, modeling what friendship truly looks like. Even more specifically, he was a spiritual coach who took the heart of a conversationalist and engaged with a high level of discernment. It was a full expression of the disciplines shared thus far, which has led me and my family to the other side of the Atlantic. Through many Skype calls and late-night conversations, something was awakened that spurred me on toward love and good deeds, giving me a sense of urgency to live a life worthy of the calling I had received.

Do you have people in your life who, just by your spending

time with them, stir you in deep ways to be a better version of yourself? Is there something within their words that awakens you to a world larger than you are already living in? A conversationalist coach may spur you on to a world going on around you, inviting you to see things in a completely new way, which allows you to pull your head up and look around with new perspective. Yet a conversationalist coach does more than just that—they act in a way that helps you articulate your response to the world you now see.

Again, Solomon says in Proverbs 20:5, "The purposes of a person's heart are deep waters, but one who has insight draws them out." A conversationalist coach does more for you internally than they do externally. Instead of only pointing to the world around you, they actually do more by asking questions to unlock what is already inside of you. This is not to any credit of the coach, but it's to give glory to what God has already placed within you. God has already given you passions, desires, and purposes that are waiting to be released—things that, for whatever reason, have been muted, diminished, or lost.

The conversationalist coach stirs the heart and brings life-giving waters to the conversation, bringing refreshment to you. This work of a spiritual coach is distinguished from what you might think of as an athletic coach or even as an executive coach. For my work, I spend time in the disciplines and the practice of coaching executives and CEOs, helping them define opportunities, overcome challenges, and find areas where they need to grow. For most discussions, this includes the organizations in which they lead, thus adding a fuller context of strategies, key initiatives, and personnel who all come together to see the vision and mission fulfilled. The more in-depth you move as a coach, the more holistic your discussion will be.

A coach may move beyond professional subjects into more personal areas, involving marriage and family, personal financial health, and social goals one hopes to achieve. Even though I do this at a vocational level, you don't have to be trained or certified as a life, executive, or athletic coach to be able to operate as a spiritual coach. Just as the first discipline suggests a confidence that you have because you have spent time with the Lord (and being with him and in his presence does something to mitigate fear and awaken faith and love within your own life), so you are able to operate from a place of confidence that helps you engage relationally. At the same time, you catch the heart of God on behalf of other people.

What is so significant about my friend Fabi is that he is a man who is deeply committed to spending time with the Lord, and by doing so his heart gets cultivated for the Lord, and then it extends to those he loves. It's during these moments where the spiritual work of encouragement and strengthening happens. It's as if courage has been imparted, where I come away from my time with him more empowered to do what I'm called to do. The discipline of spiritual coaching awakens your heart to be able to spend time with the Lord praying for your friends. As you press into the Lord on someone else's behalf, there is a discernment that is given, as well as a greater resolve to walk alongside him or her, allowing you to spur one another on toward love and good deeds.

As you look at the people in your life who have spurred you on, what can you learn from them that you can pass on to others? If you desire a greater measure of power, strength, and courage to be such a spiritual coach for others, then ask the Lord what's on his heart for your friend.

> If you desire a greater measure of power, strength, and courage to be such a spiritual coach for others, then ask the Lord what's on his heart for your friend.

When you catch God's heart for them, it will change how you are a friend. It's within this charge that you catch the urgency and worthiness of such a calling of engagement. What if, during a period of vulnerability for both Fabi and me, we would have retreated away from the honest conversations of being vulnerable with our story and a commitment to friendship? If that were the case, we would have been robbed from a blessing of strengthening and mutual encouragement.

You will achieve the kind of friendships you long for as you see others succeed in their areas of influence. The discovery process where you help unlock the secrets of people's hearts using the seven life-changing questions will bring their purposes, passions, and priorities into focus, giving them a plan to take action. Your support and strength will do more than you can imagine to help move them toward that goal. These are life-changing conversations that will result in life-changing friendships.

Discipline #6: Change: Navigating Conflict and the Challenges of Life

Whenever you are challenging the status quo, you are threatening the comfort of what is normal and predictable for the people around you. The implications of the seven life-changing questions have the potential to be disruptive. This may imply minor shifts in the circles of your relationships, or it may cause significant moves in your family or workplace. As a conversationalist, to one degree or another, you may find yourself in the space of helping navigate conflict or conflict management. Change can be traced to this principle:

Opportunities + Challenges = Growth

The moment you declare an opportunity you are going to step into, a dream that you hope to see become a reality, you are going to face some challenges. How you embrace those challenges and persevere through them will determine your growth, which ultimately enables you to engage in larger opportunities and the ability to overcome even more challenges. Growth is difficult because it represents change that, though necessary, sometimes can be difficult and costly, at least in the short term.

When I first started in my coaching work, I had the opportunity to be mentored and coached by Dr. John Townsend, the coauthor of *Boundaries*. My personal one-on-ones, as well as group coaching with him, helped me learn a lot about how to navigate growth and change with leaders. I began to observe that whenever there was a significant resolution or declaration toward a specific action, the change always seemed to be followed by conflict. In the most specific way, I learned the fact that change is hard and it's a process.

It's within this discipline of navigating conflict where you play a critical role as a conversationalist. At some point, it comes down to your ability to be a graceful truth teller. The nature of Dr. Townsend's and my relationship was one of coaching, which means he was given permission to spur me on. When he heard my ideas, rationale, or my planning, he was free to question, sharpen, and refine. It didn't feel good at the time, but it made me a better coach. His truth telling actually added value that had an exponential benefit because it extended to many conversations. He modeled a graceful truth telling that allowed me to do the same for others.

Change is hard. In fact, change and challenges often go hand in hand. Challenges produce potential conflict, and we know that conflict can either stretch our comfort zones, define new boundaries, or build bonds relationally. As conversationalists, each one of us can help guide others through the change toward one of these realities.

Truth Telling

There are many people who like the idea of being a conversationalist, who want to be invited into trustful conversations, to be inspired and to inspire others, and to catch a heart for people, moving them forward by spurring them on. Yet the moment they move in that direction, there is going to be conflict and challenges. These challenges represent a threshold in a relationship that may be a defining moment on whether or not you are willing to go there. Can you be a truth teller?

Truth telling is hard. It is hard to receive too. If you have a person who likes the feel-good side of your relationship yet cannot receive truth, then it is certainly going to limit him or her from being spurred on toward love and good works. It also limits how much truth you can speak into their life. This is critically important as you mature as a conversationalist, and it's worthy to ground this with some biblical ideas for you to think about.

As we move into this place of navigating change, there's room for graceful debate and discussion, which in the end may lead us to a place where we agree to disagree. As conversationalists, we would do well to discern the heart and response to an open rebuke. Maybe we have enjoyed a loving relationship, yet now it is at a point where we can invite some feedback and let it be done in a graceful way. This may sound something like, "Thank you so much for engaging in the conversation. Thanks for taking time to answer the questions." It may include a paraphrase or a recap to what we've heard and a request clarification in case we missed something.

Change Reveals the Heart

King David said, "Let a righteous man strike me—that is a kindness; let him rebuke me—that is oil on my head. My head will not refuse it . . . " (Psalm 141:5). Here, David is referring to the prophet Nathan's rebuke of him after his sin with Bathsheba, referring to it as kindness and oil on his head, which represents a blessing. Speaking truth may feel like a curse at times, but it is a blessing to the relationship, especially when it is extended with grace and humility.

I am an encourager, and the nature of encouragement is expressed in exhortation. So one may naturally say that I am a truth teller. But truth telling is not a license to manage, manipulate, or control relationships. I have shared things that may be truth, but I have delivered them in the wrong way and at the wrong time, and my relationships have suffered because of it. If I could do it all over again, I would have done it in a different way. The true mark of maturity is that the conversationalist knows the right balance of being able to discern when grace is required and when truth needs to be spoken.

There is no greater picture of this than Jesus's modeling of always speaking in a way that dealt with the heart. As you observe people who are on the cusp of life change, who are ready to make some choices that are hard, you can help guide them as a conversationalist by seeking wisdom for them instead of offering foolish or rash actions, help them apply and appropriate faith instead of driving them by fear. You can help them find counsel for their plans instead of acting in ignorance.

In the midst of change, understand that change may be disruptive, disappointing, and even disheartening for some people. We can help them navigate that change to minimize conflict by honoring the people in their life and by walking through the change as a process instead of an event. Conventional wisdom might suggest that conflict divides relationship, but it is in the spirit of both truth and grace that conflict actually binds friendship together through difficulty.

As you consider the challenging relationships you have, the temptation is to do whatever it takes to minimize the conflict and minimize the pain. But there is a potential of peace by persevering through the pain and difficulty of a relationship. In fact, it is the pathway toward maturity. As a conversationalist committing and walking through such a change, regardless of the difficulty and conflict, you will create the potential for lifelong friendship. And isn't that worth fighting for?

Discipline #7: Celebration: Every Victory Deserves a Party

Your role as a conversationalist can spur people on toward love and good deeds, and when they see such a dream become a reality—their plans being fulfilled and bearing fruit in their lives—it deserves more than just a pat on the back. It's worthy of celebration.

The discipline of celebration is more than a party; rather, it's an acknowledgement that stirs the heart of gratitude and mutual celebration for all people involved.

King David, in Psalm 20:4–5, declares, "May he give you the desire of your heart and make all your plans succeed. May we shout for joy over your victory and lift up our banners in the name of our God." It's a victory for which we want to be cheerleaders, declaring people's desires and helping them move forward into those desires; when they see success, we feel the same success and celebrate it. So often, desires are either forgotten in busyness or only acknowledged in the passing of a deadline so that we may be too exhausted after crossing the finish line to wave a banner of victory.

It is worthy to note that the discipline of celebration is not a new idea. It is one that is recorded throughout the Bible, marked by the word *remember*. We remember what God has done and what others have done in our lives, and so we take time to celebrate the goodness of God and the faithfulness of others. Even in the commandment of keeping the Sabbath, it is not only a day of rest but also a day to remember what the Lord your God has done for you. When we take time to remember God's work, then we reflect and appreciate what really matters most.

To listen and draw out the whispers of a desire for someone, even in moments of great timidity, and then to see such a desire walked out over time, is worthy of remembrance. Such a remembrance builds on itself over time, and as your history grows together, there is mutual celebration that says, "I remember that time that you . . . " There is an encouragement and a reminder of what has happened in the past, which actually strengthens the present and gives hope for the future.

Celebration of events that create milestones and benchmarks in our lives can be done in private with close friends, or they can be a public declaration within an organization. Even a leader who experiences a victory has the opportunity to defer some of that celebration and success on other team members, where they all share in the victory together. This gives opportunity for acknowledgement to others, because such a great victory is rarely ever done alone. Every great work is done with a team of people.

One of the greatest ways you can celebrate is by being a witness to another person's life. When it comes time, capturing a few pictures and well-timed comments and giving an acknowledgement of things you have remembered on the journey of celebrating friendship over the course of a few months or a few years, is one of the most honoring things you can do. It's telling the story of their life through your eyes, reminding them of great victory. For some of us, once we've experienced success, we have a funny way of diminishing its value or the feel of the final push. It's this work of the conversationalist that not only reminds you of victory and success but the character that was required in the hard place. It's reminding that person of how they have grown and developed.

For me, there are a few people who, with just a passing comment, would say something to the effect of, "Look where you have come in the last three years." The depth and sincerity of a comment from those who have been witnesses to my life only helps to strengthen who I am today, regardless of what I am feeling in the moment. It builds me up by reminding me to look at what we had to overcome—and if we were able to do that, then we can certainly persevere through whatever we are facing today. Think about who has shouted for you in victory when the desire of your heart was fulfilled, then think about those you have shouted for. For whom have you been a champion and cheerleader? Remember the joy and privilege it was to walk alongside them during their journey.

Write down their names, remember their stories, and send a note of encouragement reminding them of victory. Consider who in your life you should take time to celebrate, and acknowledge what the Lord has done for them. Taking time to journal a few things from their life and bringing that forward into conversation may be the encouragement they need to persevere through whatever trial they are facing. Who are the people who have found answers to one of the seven questions, and who reignited the passion of their life and are making a difference today? Who has found their strength and is operating fully energized and engaged? Who in your life has experienced such a change of heart where their attitude and sense of joy in the day-to-day is almost contagious to those around them? Who is stewarding the gifts that have been entrusted to their care? Who has had the courage to share thoughts that have never been shared? Who was once living a life in bondage and now has been freed? Who is living a life that is consistently finding new ways to bless others as they have been blessed? And who in your life has been found faithful, living a life of character, their reputation reflecting the kind of legacy they hope to leave behind?

You have no idea how such an act of consideration may be fresh water to a weary soul or healing grace for those who are broken. Those who are under the threat of discouragement may need to be encouraged, which can be done by a simple acknowledgement and celebration, reigniting the heart of gratitude and thanksgiving. This results in praise to God, as well as a renewed mind and the potential of a restored intimacy with him. Such simple celebration may be the most considerable thing you can do to spur someone on to love and good deeds.

Your Call to Action

As you mature as a conversationalist, you can grow in your ability to have a greater capacity to connect with people at a *heart* level. You may also gain access to those relationships by asking uncommon *questions* that get to the heart. However, if you don't put into practice the *disciplines* outlined in this chapter, your success will stay in your head. These seven disciplines of engagement are essential for life-changing conversations.

For each discipline, below you'll find three questions for reflection and discussion. I also provide one challenge—a call to measurable action—that will help you engage your disciplines for real life change. So far we've reflected on how we feel and we've thought about the questions we're going to ask. But now it's time for action. I'm asking you to customize your own conversationalist plan based on what is your best next step. I promise that as you engage in these calls to action, you will shape your most life-defining relationships. This is where the hard work of conversations happens, but the work is worth it, and you will be well rewarded for your commitment and efforts.

INSIGHTS AND YOUR CALL TO ACTION

Discipline #1:
Confidence: Removing the Barriers of Engagement

1. Where do you need to build confidence to overcome your fears?
2. How can you apply faith to your fears and trust God for wisdom, direction, and peace in your relationships?
3. How does time with God impact your clarity, courage, and compassion?

   ***Confidence Call to Action:* Write down one thing you can do to strengthen your confidence to affect your most important relationships. How will you make this a habit in your life?**

Discipline #2:
Circles: Defining the Who (People, Places, and Priorities)

1. Review your calendar for the past month. Where have you spent the most time in the past thirty days and with whom?
2. Where will you be traveling in the coming year? Who will be present? What could you do to intentionally prepare before you meet?
3. Whom do you need to spend less time with and what specific boundaries do you need to have in place to keep your priority relationships healthy?

Circles Call to Action: **List your top ten your priority relationships. Then write down one thing you are going to do to invest in those relationships and schedule it.**

Discipline #3: Connect: Clarifying the Expectations

1. What's the impact of a relationship with high expectations that have been consistently unmet? What's the impact of relationships with no consistent expectations?

2. Do you prefer more formal or informal relationships? How does your preferred style impact the ease or difficulty for others to engage with you?

3. What are your most recent significant conversations? Identify three of them, describing what you did to create healthy expectations. What do you learn for next time?

   Connect Call to Action: **What can you do to communicate clear expectations for your next meeting or event to honor the person you're meeting with? How can you make this a daily discipline in your life?**

Discipline #4: Considerable: Asking Great Questions

1. What are you looking forward to most in this year?

2. Using an honest self-evaluation, what are the most common questions you ask? What is the question you are most known for? How can you move from the habit of asking one cliché question to a series of considerable questions to impact your relationships positively?

3. What's the risk of asking considerable questions? What keeps *you* from asking these questions? What questions do you wish others would ask you?

   Considerable Call to Action: **Moving from the cliché "What's up?" to considerable questions, write down a list of at least ten invitational and sincere questions in your own voice that you can use each day.**

Discipline #5: Coaching: Let's Get Moving

1. Identify those in your life who do these things for you: broaden your perspective and open your world to new possibilities; give encouragement and strength; help you be a better version of yourself; help you pay attention to your priorities.
2. How do you respond to being challenged?
3. What's your style and approach to spur others to be, know, and do more with their life?

   Coaching Call to Action: What three people can you commit to spur on and be their champion and cheerleader for life change? Determine the frequency of needed engagement. Schedule a meeting to take the relationship to the next level of engagement.

Discipline #6:
Change: Navigating Conflict and the Challenges of Life

1. Why is change so hard?
2. How can people navigate change without compromising your most important relationships?
3. What changes are you currently going through that have a greater cost than you initially anticipated? What ways can you honor your most important relationships in the midst of conflict and change?

   Change Call to Action: Define specific changes you could make to take advantage of present opportunities and overcome challenges in your life?

Discipline #7: Celebration: Every Victory Deserves a Party

1. How do you celebrate someone else's success?
2. How do you like to be celebrated?
3. Why do we struggle to celebrate our own or others' accomplishments and diminish that success?

Celebration Call to Action: Who in your life has experienced a recent success that you could celebrate in a specific way? Plan and schedule that celebration. How do you want to celebrate meeting a current personal goal once it is accomplished?

Chapter 16

CONVERSATIONS THAT ECHO FOR ETERNITY: THE CALL TO DISCIPLESHIP

When I was eighteen years old, I was invited to a men's retreat in Gatlinburg, Tennessee. It was a unique setting that was designed by its leader some 10–20 years before. There were about ten guys who financially sponsored the event about a year before, then spent most of that year prayerfully considering who they would ask to come. Your ticket to the retreat was to do the twenty hours of Bible study homework, memorizing the passages that were being discussed. Those who were going to teach had to commit forty hours for their one talk. The heart engagement was preparation for the relational environment in which we met. The level of maturity, discussion, and even debate in that room still marks me to this day.

The highlight of the retreat and what is burned in my memory was the Sunday morning when the emcee asked the senior leader, Walt Hendrickson, to come to the front of the room. Kelly Talamo, who was facilitating the event, asked all the men in the room who had personally been discipled by Walt to stand up. There were about twelve guys who stood up. Then Kelly asked who had been influenced by the twelve guys who stood up to then stand, and nearly half the room stood up at this point. Then Kelly asked who had been personally influenced by these men, and the rest of the room stood.

I looked around and sensed, even at eighteen, that this was a defining moment for me. It was a picture of faithfulness, not only of one man but of many who followed behind to carry the message of the gospel and to equip others. There were about a hundred men in that room, but each of them represented families, friendships, churches, and businesses. The impact of their lives has influenced thousands, maybe even millions, around the world.

As a conversationalist, do you have a vision for what it is to be faithful to the conversations God has placed inside of you and to pass them on to others? Do you believe that your conversations have the possibility and potential to echo for eternity? Jesus gave his disciples a final charge:

> Then Jesus came to them and said, "All authority in heaven and on earth has been given to me. Therefore go and make disciples of all nations, baptizing them in the name of the Father and of the Son and of the Holy Spirit, and teaching them to obey everything I have commanded you. And surely I am with you always, to the very end of the age." (Matthew 28:18–20)

Such a charge is one to which we can respond. We are not only to make disciples, but we can have confidence that God is with us wherever we go and with whomever we engage along the way.

If discipleship is the commission, then it starts with each and every conversation we have.

In our day and age, there is a place for public proclamation, but the gospel is advanced through life conversations that extend the love of God. We are witnesses of his love and grace, and in turn we share the hope that lies within us. If discipleship is the commission, then it starts with each and every conversation we have.

The apostle Paul, when speaking to Timothy, gives us a picture of what discipleship should look like over a lifetime of faithfulness: "You then, my son, be strong in the grace that is in Christ Jesus. And the things you have heard me say in the presence of many witnesses entrust to reliable people who will also be qualified to teach others" (2 Timothy 2:1–2). How many different generations are represented in that text? First, we can see that Paul is speaking to Timothy, so that would two. Then we can see reliable men and women, which would be a third generation. Then it's that third generation who would then go on to teach others. There are four generations represented, giving us a model of what it looks like to invest our lives beyond one generation. This charge invites us to consider a life beyond ourselves. Every conversation has the potential of extending to the next circle of faithful people who will then do the same.

Standing in Gatlinburg that day as a young man, I saw a picture of these verses lived out. Though it was just a moment in time, it has marked me for a lifetime, showing me the kind of life I hope to live and the legacy I hope to leave behind, not only for my family but also for the spiritual family I hope to invest in. Conversations that echo into eternity are ones that are rooted in the Word of God, inspired by the Holy Spirit, and shared in a loving relationship. Do you believe your words can echo for eternity? Do you believe that as you are faithful to this work as a conversationalist, considering how to spur people on toward love and good deeds, you can make an eternal impact?

Maybe you have a story similar to mine—you have people who have come alongside you and who have been faithful to invest in your life, and now it's time for you to go and do the same for someone else, which extends to circles beyond your direct reach. But if this is not your story yet, it can begin today. You can see a new vision for the impact of your life by being faithful to the message and the hope inside of you. It can be passed on to others. It may be time for you to be trained, developed, and empowered for this good work. Loving others opens the door to speak to the heart, but it is the conversationalist who draws out what is already there because God has placed it there.

Wherever you are in your maturity as a conversationalist today, no matter what difficulties you have faced or disappointments that have left you hiding behind a virtual screen of relationships, keeping you from pressing forward beyond artificial responses, out there is a big world of extraordinary people living in ordinary moments. Eternity is in the hearts of those people, and you may be one question away from life change and a life-defining relationship. "Let us consider how we may spur one another on toward love and good deeds" (Hebrews 10:24). The kingdom of God is expanding, and the landscape of this kingdom is in the hearts of people. You have a calling to be an ambassador for this kingdom—you've been given everything you need.

Love as you have been loved, spur others on as you have been spurred on, and encourage others as you have been encouraged. Be faithful to the good work as you have seen others be faithful. Your work as an ambassador for the kingdom of God begins with an invitation. It's an invitation into conversation. Your conversation may echo the very words of the grace of God that are extended by this invitation, because as an ambassador you are introducing them to the King of kings and Lord of lords. The love and good deeds of your life are the good news of the gospel of Christ being expressed through faithfulness and love.

The greatest life change comes with a conversation with Jesus Christ. Together, as your conversation grows in depth and maturity with the Savior of your soul, you will know what it is to be loved. For it is out of this love that you will be able to extend love to others. Not only will your life be transformed, but a transformation will take place in your relationships as well. That transformation can begin today with one conversation. Who will you love well? Who will be blessed by your good works? One conversation may echo for all eternity.

Appendix

Fifty Questions of a Conversationalist

1. What's one thing about you I don't know?

2. What's the important thing going on in your world right now?

3. What are you looking forward to most this year?

4. What do you do with your free time?

5. What's your favorite vacation spot?

6. What books have you read more than once?

7. What's the most significant challenge you've faced in the last year?

8. What have you learned from your _____ experience?

9. What can I do to help?

10. What do you want to do when you grow up?

11. Where do you hope to retire?

12. Where did you grow up?

13. Where did you go to school?

14. Where was your first job?

15. Where were you when _____? (For example, when Y2K happened or when 9/11 took place.)

16. Where have you traveled?

17. Where would you like to visit?

18. Where do you work?

19. Where do you hope to be in a year?

20. Where's your favorite place in the world?

21. Where has your dream met reality?

22. How do you work through disappointment?

23. Where does your passion get expressed today?

24. What's the impact you hope to see from your life?

25. What assumptions are you making about your current life situation that might not be valid?

26. What or who are you blaming for holding you back in life?

27. At this point in your life, who do you most want to help do what?

28. Who do you no longer want to help?

29. What will this change cost you? What will it cost you if you don't make the change?

30. What would your life look like if you could make a few changes? What would those changes be?

31. How would you define a "good friend"?

32. Do you have a friend who fits that definition? How about you as a friend?

33. What are two practices that help you grow in your love and intimacy with Jesus when you engage them?

34. When did you become a man or woman?

35. What are the three most challenging issues in your life today?

36. What is your story?

37. If you could change one thing in your world today, what would it be?

38. What are you really good at? What comes natural to you?

39. If you were to fail, in what three areas are you most vulnerable?

40. Who in your life are you still working to forgive?

41. What really brings or gives you life?

42. What is your greatest regret so far in life?

43. What are three exciting things that have already happened in your life?

44. If you could write a book about one chapter in your life, what would it be?

45. How are you experiencing God at this time in your life?

46. What do you think God is doing in your life right now?

47. When have you last seen the fingerprints of God in your life?

48. How can I pray for you?

49. Can you think of a time where you knew God was real and working in your life?

50. What comes into your mind when you think about God?

ACKNOWLEDGMENTS

The Conversationalist begins and ends with my faith and gratitude to my Lord and Savior Jesus Christ, who modeled a life of asking questions that went straight to the heart.

This book is a sum of a lifetime of relationships. The greatest treasure of my life is my sweetheart and best friend, Cari. There is no doubt this project would have ever happened without her love, support, and ability to transcribe words in these pages that she drew right from my heart. My daughter Ellie desires deep, meaningful relationships. Her comment on one of our hiking dates that "no one knows how to ask questions anymore" inspired me to write the book. My daughter Bethany has a gift of the creative that stirred my heart and relit me again and again when I needed a spark. My son Grady's constant laughter and humor brought me joy. I loved it when he asked, "Daddy, do I have to be a conversationalist now?" And I replied, "You've got a gift son. You'll far exceed your dad." *The Conversationalist* started with my family and I pray it continues with many life-changing questions that will lead to life-defining relationships.

To all my extended family, thank you for your prayers, encouragement, and love over a lifetime.

To all my mentors, thank you for asking the questions and modeling the life of a conversationalist. Galatians 6:6 says, "The one who receives instruction in the word should share all good things with their instructor." To Paul and Phyllis Stanley, your investment in me started through writing in 1994 with "Connecting" and hundreds of conversations since. Dave Jewitt, I found my One Degree. A special thanks to my friend Michael Brunner, greasy eggs and terrible coffee make for great conversations. Peter Jackson, what an adventure for twenty-five years. I'm so grateful for a friendship that started over football at the Fellowship Bible Church men's retreat. Gary Mcloughlin, the Irish moors are deep in my soul. Richard Mace, you stood with me during my transition from Georgia to Colorado; you've been my conversational advocate and good friend. Boyd Bailey, you're one of the greatest conversationalists that I've ever met whose sensitivity to God's leading opened the doors for my life work with leaders. Chris Duncan and Marc Ottestad, you believed in me and helped get the conversation going with leaders. To my friends at Convene, what a privilege to have walked with you and learned from your examples to spur on leaders to love and good deeds.

To my Advance leadership team, you are my friends, allies, and advocates for *The Conversationalist*. Our CEO team was the birthplace of what it means to be a conversationalist and we lived it out during our forum days. Thank you, Ed, Vance, Cris, Scott, Jason, Kevin, Austin, Ken, Conor, Daniel, Tim, Pete, Dale, Matt, and Bob. To my key leader team, thank you for eighteen months of forum-day conversations and your grace to give me the break I needed to get the book completed.

To my pastors and friends at New Life Church in Colorado Springs, thank you for the grace of community and family marked by life-defining conversations that have been felt all over the world.

To the team at BroadStreet Publishing, Carlton and David, thanks for giving me a shot.

To my friends in Colorado Springs and Georgia (and circles around the world), thanks for the heart, the questions, and the disciplines that shaped all our conversations.

For all future conversationalists, thanks for having the courage to engage. You inspire me to do the same!

ABOUT THE AUTHOR

RUSSELL VERHEY is an entrepreneur, leadership advocate, and consultant walking alongside leaders in coaching discussions that result in life and organizational change. He facilitates leadership forums that engage and develop stronger leaders, producing greater team alignment, engagement, and synergy. Russell is the president of The Advance and hold a master's degree in leadership development. He and his wife with their four children make their home in Colorado Springs, Colorado.

RussellVerhey.com
Twitter: @russellverhey
Facebook.com/russell.verhey
Linkedin.com/in/russellverhey